PENGUIN (P) CLASSICS

THE THREEPENNY OPERA

BERTOLT BRECHT was born in Augsburg, Bavaria, in 1898 and left Germany in 1933 when Hitler came to power. He lived in the United States for seven years, settling with his family in Santa Monica and New York, and continuing to work on plays and films. After the war, Brecht returned to Germany, where he founded the Berliner Ensemble. He died in 1956.

NADINE GORDIMER is the author of over twelve novels, as well as numerous collections of stories and essays. She has received many awards, including the Booker Prize (for *The Conservationist* in 1974) and the Nobel Prize in Literature in 1991. She lives in Johannesburg, South Africa.

NORMAN ROESSLER, PhD, is editor of *Communications,* the performance journal of the International Brecht Society, and is a lecturer at Temple University in Philadelphia, Pennsylvania.

BERTOLT BRECHT

The Threepenny Opera

Foreword by
NADINE GORDIMER

Introduction to the Penguin Classics Edition by
NORMAN ROESSLER

Translated and Edited with an Introduction by
RALPH MANHEIM AND JOHN WILLETT

PENGUIN BOOKS

PENGUIN BOOKS

Published by the Penguin Group

Penguin Group (USA) Inc., 375 Hudson Street, New York, New York 10014, U.S.A. • Penguin Group (Canada),
90 Eglinton Avenue East, Suite 700, Toronto, Ontario, Canada M4P 2Y3 (a division of Pearson Penguin Canada
Inc.) • Penguin Books Ltd, 80 Strand, London WC2R 0RL, England • Penguin Ireland, 25 St Stephen's Green,
Dublin 2, Ireland (a division of Penguin Books Ltd) • Penguin Group (Australia), 250 Camberwell Road, Cam-
berwell, Victoria 3124, Australia (a division of Pearson Australia Group Pty Ltd) • Penguin Books India Pvt
Ltd, 11 Community Centre, Panchsheel Park, New Delhi – 110 017, India • Penguin Group (NZ), 67 Apollo
Drive, Rosedale, North Shore 0632, New Zealand (a division of Pearson New Zealand Ltd) • Penguin Books
(South Africa) (Pty) Ltd, 24 Sturdee Avenue, Rosebank, Johannesburg 2196, South Africa

Penguin Books Ltd, Registered Offices:
80 Strand, London WC2R 0RL, England

First published in Great Britain by Eyre Methuen Ltd. 1979
First published in the United States of America by Arcade Publishing, Inc. 1994
Published by arrangement with Arcade Publishing, Inc.
This edition with a foreword by Nadine Gordimer and introductions by
Norman Roessler published in Penguin Books 2007

15   17   19   20   18   16   14

LIBRARY OF CONGRESS CATALOGING IN PUBLICATION DATA
Brecht, Bertolt, 1898–1956.
[Dreigroschenoper. English]
The threepanny opera / Bertolt Brecht ; transalted and edited by Ralph Manheim and John Willert ;
foreword by Nadine Gordimer ; introduction by Norman Roessler.
p. cm—(penguin classics)
ISBN 978-0-14-310516-9
I. Manheim, Ralph, 1907–   II. Willett, John.   III. Title.
PT2603.R397D7513   2008
832'.912—dc22   2007040164

Printed in the United States of America

Contents

Foreword

Some works of the imagination—novels, plays—illuminate in the beam of their time; one can click back onto them for a deep understanding of an era that no historical account can convey. These works capture the past but belong to the past's confine. There are others that have innate prescience—which will become amazingly relevant to different eras and places. Let's not cite the obvious: Greek drama, Shakespeare, Chekhov, Ibsen. It's a matter of the masters of the theater never being out of date in the human theater of existential responses. When different centuries and different resources of human intelligence, scientific invention, ingenuity change the world—how did genius writers know that we would have to tackle survival with only the same amour of the spirit, the same moral choices, no matter the scope of human activity? It's not because the world doesn't change; it doesn't change enough. Not in terms of human fulfillment.

We've walked on the moon but the poor still inhabit the earth.

Bertolt Brecht heard of John Gay's *The Beggar's Opera* through his collaborator as translator of foreign works into his native German, Elisabeth Hauptmann. Gay's early eighteenth-century social and political satire, using English traditional songs in parody of Italian grand opera inspired Brecht as a tool of theater he could handle to create modes he was experimenting with in his early plays as revelation of the state of his own time and place, Germany in the 1920s. Gay's subject—or rather send-up—was engorged aristocracy; his antihero a highwayman:

two sides of criminality proposed, meeting only in corruption—
"A rich rogue nowadays is fit company for any gentleman."
This inversion of contemporary morals was exactly what
Brecht was thrusting in the face of his audience with *The
Threepenny Opera* two hundred years later, a people exploited
by different forms of authority in a chaotic industrialized time
and ethos. Hauptmann translated Gay's anti-opera and Brecht
reconceived the theme that was already within him—a working
purpose as raison d'être—out of the alienation he was living
through, the aftermath of Germany's defeat in World War I. A
class of rich industrialists, entrepreneurs, were enabled to revive
their old lifestyle with backing from their opportunist counter-
parts in international finance, enemies turned capitalist brother-
under-the-skin, while the general population, unemployed,
barely survived starvation. Their messiah had already pro-
claimed himself in a Munich beer hall. Adolph Hitler. The
wide-screen of Hitler's rise from there to power is the real backdrop of the first staging of the *The Threepenny Opera*, Berlin
1928, the year halfway to his accession as Chancellor of Germany in 1933.

The Threepenny Opera's Macheath is Mac the Knife, skilled
city crime operator as well as highwayman, and the cast of
other characters, with minor changes, is that of Gay's play.
Jonathan Jeremiah Peachum is the proprietor of a rather special
outfitting shop; outfits that will make beggars of various kinds
catch the eye, touch the hearts—and pockets—of the public.
He's a fence—forerunner of Fagan? But of a higher underclass,
so to speak. Peachum and his wife have a beautiful daughter,
Polly, whom they lovingly cherish—as a piece of prime goods
they'll profit by when they make some sexual alliance with a
wealthy man for her. They're a comic couple Brecht uses to de-
light us with our own awful laughter at the outrageous. Polly's
form of counter-revolt against the inversion of conventional
morality is involuntary—she's fallen in love with Mac the
Knife. Secretly, the wedding is taking place at a venue occupied
illegally, like everything else appropriated in Mac's life, in a stable on the property of no less than the Duke of Devonshire. An

honored guest is Tiger Brown, High Sheriff and undercover buddy of Mac the Knife.

Falling in love has no place in the city jungle of the poor. "If you're immoral enough to get married, did it have to be a horse-thief and highwayman?" Mrs. Peachum berates her daughter when the marriage is discovered. And her father adds "To a notorious criminal," meanwhile distracted by his own illicit dealings, arguing with a beggar who complains that the fake stump of limb he's bought is a botch-up. Mother and father have a solution to their daughter's betrayal. Report the son-in-law's whereabouts to the police; he's a man wanted for many crimes. "That way" says Peachum, "we get him hanged free of charge . . . Two birds with one stone"—the husband disposed of without paying someone to do the job. Mrs. Peachum knows where he is to be found. "He's holed up with his tarts."

Peachum: "But they won't turn him in."

"Just let me attend to that . . ."

Polly tells dear mama to save herself the trouble. If Mac is arrested, in the prison the Sheriff would "serve him a cocktail; they'd smoke their cigars and have a little chat about a certain shop in this street where a little more goes on than meets the eye." Even if Polly has broken the outlaw code by falling in love, a sentimentality only the soft life of the rich can afford, she has been properly brought up: in necessity she'll turn in her own outfitting dear father.

The ruthless alternative codes of human relationships the poor must adhere to for their survival are extolled by the trio, father, mother, and daughter breaking into song, music-hall style.

> Who wouldn't like an earthly paradise?
> Yet our condition's such it can't arise
> . . . We should aim high instead of low
> But our condition's such this can't be so
> . . . The world is poor, and man's a shit
> And that's all there is to it.

Mac the Knife is indeed betrayed, by Jenny, his favorite in his brothel haunt, and his occupation of a prison cell is further complicated by his multiple entanglements with women who turn up at the prison and have what must be one of the most witty, savage, and subtle exchanges of words in the history of satire. Both have common purpose in wanting to save Mac's life and both want to save him—each for herself. Will the rogue bargain his escape as would only be expected of him? Or shall we see him strung up? Brecht, in his revolutionary mission of what he termed "estrangement," casts into some prop room the emotional resolution modes of bourgeois theater that offer the audience easy empathy or indignation, and parodies both by handing over to the audience, in this case the reader, the decision of which end would be believable in terms of the reality they know in their own time and place. Like any important slave plantation owner in the appropriate past, any loyal financial tycoon supporting trade barriers to keep out competition from other countries in the present, Mac the Knife is honored instead of condemned. A well-endowed royal pardon arrives. Of the plight of dire human circumstance in general, it's Mrs. Peachum who seems to have the last word. "How nice and easy everything would be if you could always reckon with saviours on horseback."

And how easy it would have been for Bertolt Brecht to idealize his poor and downtrodden in attack on both the bourgeoisie and the deadly genocidal dictatorship that succeeded it in Germany. But he does not allow himself to distort what his genius gave him the clarity to face: that social degradation, the stripping of human dignity, creates the nakedness of cruelty between the victims themselves. Is it the sole mode of behavior, for survival? Milan Kundera has said "Writers don't give answers, they ask questions." Jenny and Mac the Knife sing a duet with an answer:

> You gentlemen who think you have a mission
> To purge us of the seven deadly sins
> Should first sort out the basic food position
> Then start your preaching: that's where it begins . . .

Food is the first thing. Morals follow on.
So first make sure that whose who now are starving
Get proper helpings when we do the carving.

Reading this dazzling, accusatory, audacious play is strangely exhilarating—which is Brecht's triumph. Not didactic, not tract: the swift rhythms and poetic wit jolt one into new confrontation with our own conditioning in our own time, when corruption is the code, from slipping a petty sum to the traffic cop who tears up the speeding ticket to bribing the member of government with millions to ensure acceptance of an arms deal. Ours is a twenty-first century when the class divide between rich and poor nations is in reality the abyss where the poor have their habitation, despite our humanistic euphemisms, Jenny the whore become Sex Worker, poverty become Underdevelopment, Globalization the term for sharing out humankind's resources among the most powerful nations.

Kurt Weill's music is not an accompaniment to Brecht's play, of course, but intrinsic to its conception: the "estrangement" in song between the lovely melody and the recitative. Hearing Weill's music is what's missing from reading the text of the play, but the text is a marvelous performance in itself, a spectacle created in the third eye of the reader's roused imagination. Maybe the publication of Brecht's splendid revelation in this new edition will wake up producers and directors to stage the play anew, against the present backdrop, while our contemporary world does the carving.

NADINE GORDIMER

Introduction to the
Penguin Classics Edition

BERTOLT BRECHT

First comes eating and then comes morality.

Staring is not seeing.

Thinking is one of the chief pleasures of the human race.

Whether reading or viewing the work of the German artist
Bertolt Brecht (1898–1956), one is greeted by a series of titles, gestures, images, aphorisms—like those listed above—
which may be written on placards lowered from the rafters,
projected on film screens, expressed through the performative
body, or delivered with a hammerlike thud on the written
page. On a linguistic, aesthetic, and philosophical level these
effects are meant to pull the reader out of a passive and un-
conscious state of mind and into a heightened condition of
awareness that leads to an alternative way of thinking and
acting in the world. Such devices were just one element of
Brecht's notion of a dialectical theater—a performance experience which explored, examined, and challenged traditional
ideas of Western aesthetic philosophy as well as confronted
the most important political and historical issues of the day in
an intensely intellectual, oftentimes contradictory, yet always
pleasurable manner.

To be good, yet live.

War teaches people nothing.

*Whoever empathizes with someone, and does so completely, re-
linquishes criticism both of the object of their empathy and of*

themselves. Instead of awakening, they sleepwalk. Instead of doing something, they let something be done with them.

At the dawn of the twenty-first century, as the terrible landmarks of the previous century (the Holocaust, world wars, the nuclear age) lose their immediacy and power, and the new century brings new monuments to our world (9/11, ethnic cleansing, global warming), we find Brecht, who seemed so absolutely determined by the twentieth century and hence rendered null and void by its end, to be even more relevant. For Brecht, although a product of the "dark times" of the twentieth century, nevertheless was not imprisoned by the era that he lived in. Brecht mediated his times through the grander lens of Western history, philosophy, and aesthetics; hence, Brecht provides not just a conversation with the twentieth century, but a dialogue which reaches back through Nietzsche, Ibsen, Marx, Shakespeare, Aristotle, Sophocles, and Socrates and forward to our current postmodern epoch. Moreover, it is not a simple conversation Brecht provides, but rather an elegant puzzle that includes the constant sting of the irritating gadfly. At every moment when we experience theater, film, music, art, video games, we feel the jab of Brecht asking us to stay awake, retain our critical faculties, conceive our existence in an aesthetic way, and finally intervene and change the world that we have constructed—because our life depends on it.

The proof of the pudding lies in the eating.

The philosophers have in various ways only interpreted the world; the point, however, is to change it.

ORIGINS

I have always needed the spur of contradiction.

Brecht was born in Augsburg, Germany (southwestern Germany, near Munich) in 1898 to comfortable middle-class parents, and he enjoyed a fairly normal childhood. Often sickly, and an inattentive student at school, he found early inspiration in the work of writers such as Villon, Rimbaud, and Wedekind, and as a result, produced a number of poems, songs, and play fragments throughout his youth. One of his earliest school friends from this period, Caspar Neher, would later design many of the stages for Brecht's theatrical work. Neither military service as a medical orderly at the end of World War I nor a brief university education (one semester) at the University of Munich decisively affected his life, but in the same year (1918) he did finish his first play, *Baal*. Until 1924, he would be based largely in Munich (with several important trips to Berlin), a period in which he would establish important relationships with Herbert Ihering (Berlin theater critic) and Helene Weigel (Jewish-Austrian, Marxist actor, and future wife) and write plays that would define his early career: *Drums in the Night* (1919), *In the Jungle of the Cities* (1922), as well as work with the material that would become *A Man's a Man* (1926). *Drums in the Night* would be his first play to be produced on the stage in September 1922 at the Munich Kammerspiele; when it premiered in Berlin in December of the same year it proved to be a decisive impetus for his career.

Brecht moved to Berlin in 1924, where he would be based until 1933, and as the Golden Age of the Weimar Republic played out, he would elevate his career to an international level. The Weimar Republic (the Roaring Twenties for an American audience) was the collective name given to the political society of Germany between the end of World War I (1918) and the rise of Adolf Hitler (1933). The Weimar Republic, similar to the French Revolution of the eighteenth century, is both a primer and cautionary tale about a western, democratic, and capitalist culture that extends itself too far and descends into decadence, chaos, hyperinflation, and ultimately totalitarian dictatorship. It was during this period that Brecht established a collaborative relationship with both Elisabeth Hauptmann and Kurt Weill, worked with two famous directors (Max Reinhardt at the Deutsches Theater and Erwin Piscator at his Dramaturgical

Collective), turned intellectually and politically to Marxism, and published a groundbreaking book of poems *Hauspostille* (*Domestic Breviary*). *The Threepenny Opera* premiered in August 1928 at the Theater am Schiffbauerdamm in Berlin, which would later become the home theater of Brecht's theater collective, the Berliner Ensemble (BE), after World War II. The premiere was a huge success, catapulting Brecht and Weill to national and international fame. *The Threepenny Opera* moment is often seen as both the high point and fall of the Weimar Republic. With the onset of the Great Depression in October 1929, the Weimar Republic quickly descended into political and cultural chaos, which would eventually see the rise of Hitler and the Nazi Party. In the last years of the Weimar Republic, Brecht would continue his collaborative work with Hauptmann and Weill and establish new collaborative relationships with Margarete Steffin, Hanns Eisler, and Slatan Dudow, which would produce works such as the opera *Mahagonny*, the film *Kuhle Wampe*, and didactic plays such as *The Measures Taken*. Hitler became chancellor on January 30, 1933, and consolidated power through numerous acts of political terror, including the infamous Reichstag Fire of February 28, 1933. Brecht, as the writer of *The Threepenny Opera*, with announced Marxist leanings, was on the short list of Nazi enemies, and hence, a day after the Reichstag Fire, wasted no time fleeing into exile.

In exile, Brecht would take up residence in various countries: Denmark, 1933–1939; Sweden, 1939–1940; Finland, 1940–1941, and the United States, 1941–1947. Operating without a native language, stage, culture, or audience, Brecht nevertheless was able to produce theoretical, theatrical, and poetic work that has come to define his later career. In Denmark he established a collaborative relationship with Ruth Berlau, thus completing (along with Helene Weigel, Elisabeth Hauptmann, and Margarete Steffin) what contemporary scholarship, based on John Fuegi's 1994 book *Brecht & Co.: Sex, Politics, and the Making of the Modern Drama* has come to understand as Brecht's inner circle. This inner circle, Brecht & Co., has been defined in various ways: at its best, as a free, fluid, and equal collaborative ensemble, which accepted the single designation of "Brecht" for collaborative work; at its worst, an exploitative / parasitic relationship, in which Brecht, through sex and charisma, rendered invisible the authorship and voice of his female collaborators. This conundrum of Brecht & Co. brings up the issue of authorship—whether the work of art is ever just the effort of one person, or whether single authorship ultimately is based on the necessity of granting authorship to one individual instead of a group. Brecht is an extreme version of this problem, because his aesthetic works are monuments to fluidity, i.e. constantly being written and rewritten and hence never stable.

Beginning in 1938 / 1939 (as the Holocaust was prefigured through Kristallnacht, November 9, 1938, and the beginning of World War II with the invasion of Poland, September 1, 1939) Brecht would produce his great, mature works: *Galileo, Good Person of Szechwan, Mother Courage and Her Children, The Messingkauf Dialogues, The Resistible Rise of Arturo Ui,* and *The Caucasian Chalk Circle.* After the end of World War II he stayed in the United States for an additional two years waiting to see what would happen in Germany and whether he could make it in the American theater and film industry. In October 1947, he was called to testify before the House Un-American Activities Committee (HUAC), which was investigating communist and anti-American activity. To the dismay of many, he did not invoke his right not to testify and instead performed an ambivalent piece of political theater, which in the end left everyone confused. This was his swan song in America, and he embarked the following day for Switzerland.

With the successful premiere of *Mother Courage* (with his wife Helene Weigel in the lead role) at the Deutsches Theater in Berlin as well as the publication of *A Short Organum for the Theatre* (a distillation of the *Messingkauf Dialogues*) in January 1949, Brecht successfully reintroduced himself back into the European theater scene. Germany was now a divided country, the concrete and symbolic center of the Cold War conflict between the United States and the Soviet Union, a situation which would last until 1990 when Germany was reunified.

Brecht settled in East Berlin (yet kept his Austrian passports and Swiss bank accounts), eventually founding, along with Helene Weigel, his own theater company, The Berliner Ensemble (BE), in 1949. In the last years of his life he worked to bring all his theatrical work to the post-war audience, and at the same time attempted to negotiate the ambivalences of the Cold War. Beginning in 1954, the BE undertook a series of guest residencies throughout Europe, and it was these tours that thrust the BE and Brecht's theatrical work back into the international scene. He died in August 1956.

Over the last fifty years, Brecht has continued to play the Socratic gadfly, fascinating and irritating us at the same time. Epic theater, alienation effects, gestus, anti-Aristotelian, mimesis, empathy, illusion, psychological / social, dissonance—all these terms (and more) comprise the aesthetic philosophy of Brecht, and are rendered in this edition (and increasingly in scholarship) through the summary term "dialectical theater," a term Brecht himself used more and more at the end of his career. In short, dialectical theater resists absolutes, essentials, and identifications and instead seeks out contradictions, diversities, and multiplicities. Nothing is eternal, all is fluid, and so, ultimately all is changeable. In dialectical theater, the writer, actor, and spectator are consciously and cognitively involved in the performance they are collectively creating. This position stands in contrast to the main tradition of Western performance, what Brecht referred to as the Aristotelian tradition, in which one is asked to identify, empathize, and lose oneself to the illusion and mystery of the performance. In his theatrical works, but especially in his theoretical writings, Brecht explored this idea of dialectical theater. Indeed, what distinguishes Brecht most is his philosophical-theoretical work which accompanies his performance work. Brecht left behind extensive aesthetic writings, contained in seven volumes in the standard edition of his complete works in German, yet these writings do not form a systematic or even consistent expression of an aesthetic theory. What Brecht gives us in his theoretical and theatrical writings are political and aesthetic puzzles, which are meant to stimulate awareness and critical thinking, and which Brecht believed were necessary and pleasurable endeavors within the human condition.

THE PROOF OF THE PUDDING: READING BRECHT

"The proof of the pudding lies in the eating" was a favored motto of Brecht and constantly reminded him that performance was about actions and not about theories. In this introduction, much has been said about Brecht's art, but how does all this theoretical commentary translate into actually reading Brecht? The text as a work of art is never a destination, but a portal experience. This is especially true of the performance text and, above all, true of the Brechtian performance text. Here are some of the portals that the reader should consider when reading these editions of Brecht in translation: 1) the primary playscripts and their variations; 2) the secondary material that accompanies the playscript: theoretical ruminations, dramaturgical explanations, and photo descriptions; 3) the musical "text" contained within the playscript—songs and compositions; 4) extension of the playscript into other genres—theoretical essay, novel, film adaptation; 5) the significant global theatrical productions over the last fifty years; 6) the translations and adaptations into different languages.

When reading Brecht, one should keep these portals in mind as accompaniment in the reading of the primary text. For example, when reading the primary playscript, one should not be afraid to use the secondary material located in the back of the text as part of the performance material. Stopping one's reading in mid-piece to consult another text is Brechtian in itself, and perusing the theoretical material and the questions and contradictions that they bring up will expand the puzzle of the text. Also, keep in mind that the Willett / Manheim translations used in this edition are not the only translations, and others from Eric Bentley, Tony Kushner, or David Hare (to name just a few) will show different ways of rendering the text. The image, or the description of the image from a historical production (e.g. Helene Weigel's "silent scream" in *Mother Courage*, Martin Wuttke contorting himself into a human swastika in *Arturo Ui*), and the sound of a song in various renditions (e.g. "Mac the Knife" from *The Threepenny Opera* sung by Kurt Gerron, Bertolt Brecht, Scott Merrill, Bobby Darrin, Sting, or Cyndi Lauper or the "Alabama Song" from *Mahagonny* sung by Lotte Lenya, Jim Morrison, or Marilyn Manson) are all methods of constructing a richer experience.

THE THREEPENNY OPERA

First comes eating and then comes morality

Brutal, scandalous, perverted, yet humorous, hummable, with a happy ending—and at the beginning of the twenty-first century utterly ubiquitous. The *Threepenny Opera* has become such a part of the DNA of Western cultural imagination that it is almost impossible to unpack anymore. The most common response to any theatrical revival is a sense of déjà vu. In the realm of musical theater we recognize *The Threepenny Opera* when we view Stephen Sondheim's *Sweeney Todd* or the *Rocky Horror Picture Show*; in the arena of theatrical music we recognize Frank Zappa's *Joe's Garage* and Tom Waits's *Swordfishrombones*; in the realm of pop music we hear the song "Mac the Knife" in the voice of Louis Armstrong, Bobby Darin, Frank Sinatra, and Ella Fitzgerald; in the character Mac the Knife, we recognize the celebrity gangster with an existential view on life such as Michael Corleone. Hence, when we see a revival of *The Threepenny Opera* and feel a sense of déjà vu, it is not just that we have seen or heard it before; it is that we see and hear it all the time in our cultural life. Such is the achievement and challenge of *The Threepenny Opera*. By the time he wrote *Mother Courage* a decade later, Brecht better understood how to negotiate the difficult terrain between cultural criticism and cultural pornography, but in *The Threepenny Opera*, the jury is, so to speak, still out. As one explores this work one should keep the following quote from the "Second Threepenny Finale" in mind, and reflect on whether it is a call to arms or a car crash that we cannot stop looking at:

> *What keeps mankind alive? The fact that millions*
> *Are daily tortured, stifled, punished, silenced, oppressed.*
> *Mankind can keep alive thanks to its brilliance*
> *In keeping its humanity repressed.*
> *For once you must try not to shirk the facts:*
> *Mankind is kept alive by bestial acts.*

STORY

The Threepenny Opera is the story of Macheath, or Mac the Knife, and his rise, fall, and (with the help of deus ex machina) rise again. King of the Victorian-era London underworld and its pimps, whores, murderers, and thieves, Macheath is, as the opening number "Mac the Knife" tells us, a murderer, rapist, and arsonist. He does battle, on the eve of the queen's coronation, with the King of the Beggars, Jonathan Peachum. Macheath, not just a vicious criminal, but an intelligent, seductive, and sensual one who has captured the heart of Peachum's daughter, Polly, whom he marries without Peachum's consent. Enraged at this attack on his property rights and economic sphere of influence, Peachum forces Tiger Brown, the chief constable of London and old army buddy of Macheath, to seek Macheath's arrest and execution. Betrayed by his whore Jenny, Macheath is arrested not once, but twice, and is sent to the gallows. Immediately before his execution, a messenger rides in and grants him a pardon, a title of nobility, a castle, and a pension. If this exercise in plot summary strikes the reader as absurd, i.e. both the content and the recapitulation of the content, then the reader has fully grasped the revolutionary impact of the play. Brecht & Co. not only constructed a play about terrible people who engage in inhuman practices, but a really bad story about terrible people who engage in inhuman practices, yet it proved irresistibly and irritatingly compelling.

ORIGINS

The origins, development, and production of *The Threepenny Opera* are a model study of the collaborative ensemble, "Brecht & Co." Closely adapted from John Gay's original *The Beggar's Opera* (1728) by Elisabeth Hauptmann, with music by Kurt Weill, and texts and lyrics by Brecht (who liberally used poems by Francois Villon and Rudyard Kipling), one can no longer simply give sole, or perhaps even primary, credit to Brecht for the work. Brecht / Weill / Hauptmann / Gay (or some variation of this listing) would be the most honest way to express authorship. In 1926, Elisabeth Hauptmann first heard of revivals of John Gay's *The Beggar's Opera* successfully playing on English stages since 1920. She quickly translated the playscript and libretto and gave it to Brecht, who acknowledged it but was preoccupied with various other projects. A chance meeting with Ernst-Joseph Aufricht, an actor who had recently come into a large inheritance and wanted to open a new show at the Theater am Schiffbauerdamm (later to become the home of the Berliner Ensemble) gave Brecht the opportunity to develop the play for a premiere in late August 1928. Brecht brought the up-and-coming composer Kurt Weill on board, and Brecht, Weill, and Hauptmann began work on the music and libretto. Working throughout the summer of 1928 right up through rehearsals (with director Erich Engels) to the premiere on August 31, 1928, the collaborators barely delivered a finished product.

"Mac the Knife," written a few days before the premiere, opened the show, but both the song and the first couple of scenes seemed to have little effect on the audience. However, with the ferocious "Cannon Song," the audience embraced the production wholeheartedly, and the result was a smashing success that would spread throughout Germany and Europe over the next several years. The success led to a soundtrack released in 1930, and a film contract from Nero Films for which Brecht wrote a treatment entitled *The Bruise*. Disagreements between Nero Films and Brecht and Weill on the cinematic adaptation led to both authors withdrawing from the project after a financial settlement was reached. The film, directed by G. W. Pabst was released in 1931, and met with solid success. Brecht would continue to develop the *Threepenny* material over the next two decades, resulting in the published playscript with additions to the original 1928 version (1931), a sociological essay, "The Threepenny Lawsuit" (1931), and *The Threepenny Novel* (1933/34), and new versions, and additional verses and song versions (1946–1948). Brecht's final additions were not agreed to by Weill, and the Weill estate would eventually publish its own standard edition of the play based on the 1928 premiere (2000).

PERFORMANCE HISTORY

When the Nazis came to power in 1933, *The Threepenny Opera* was banned and although performed in some locations during the 1930s and 1940s, it did not enjoy a renaissance until the 1950s. In 1952, Marc Blitzstein adapted the play in English, and this adaptation was first performed at Brandeis University in 1952 under the direction of Leonard Bernstein. This successful staging led to a production in March 1954 at the Theater de Lys in New York City's Greenwich Village (now named the Lucille Lortel Theatre, which would also be the site of the 1961 production of *Brecht on Brecht* which, along with *Threepenny*, was the primary dissemination of Brecht in America in the 1960s). Starring Scott Merril, Charlotte Rae, and Bea Arthur, as well as Kurt Weill's widow, Lotte Lenya, *The Threepenny Opera* was a success but was forced to close early due to a scheduling conflict. With sales of the original cast soundtrack climbing and pressure from the *New York Times* theater critic Brooks Atkinson, the production returned to the theater in September 1955 and ran until December 1961, establishing the record at that time for an off-Broadway run.

In 1956, two important productions were mounted: one in London, England, directed by Sam Wanamaker and one in Milan, Italy, directed by Giorgio Strehler. The London production used the Blitzstein adaptation and was able to convince London theatergoers of the merit of Brecht & Co.'s interpretation of John Gay's original work. The latter production was notable in that Brecht attended the last rehearsals, sharing his thoughts with Strehler (excerpted transcripts of their conversation are included in this volume) as well as the successful premiere in which Brecht made numerous curtain calls. In 1960, Brecht's own company, the Berliner Ensemble produced its first version of the play with the original director of the 1928 production, Erich Engels, at the helm. In 1963, a second *Threepenny* film was released in German and English, starring Curt Jürgens and Sammy Davis, Jr., but was met with a lukewarm reception.

The next stage of *Threepenny* productions emerged in the mid-1970s with the June 1976 production at the Vivian Beaumont Theater in New York City produced by Joseph Papp and the New York Shakespeare Festival (forerunner of the current Public Theatre) under the direction of the avant-garde theater director Richard Foreman. Starring Raul Julia and using the then-new Manheim / Willett translation, it ran successfully for over six months, garnering numerous Tony Awards and sending the still undiscovered American playwright Tony Kushner (*Angels in America*) back to the show numerous times.

In the 1980s, notable productions emerged in London in 1986 (with Tim Curry of *Rocky Horror Picture Show* fame as Macheath), Paris in 1986 (with director Giorgio Strehler revisiting the play), Berlin in 1987 (with director Gunter Krämer), and New York City in 1989 (with rock star Sting as Macheath), of which only the Strehler and Krämer productions achieved any type of popular or critical success. The 1990s saw three notable productions: in Frankfurt am Main in 1994 (using Weill's original score performed by Ensemble Modern), in London in 1994 (with a new adaptation by Robert David MacDonald and Jeremy Sams), and in 1999 a new musical soundtrack was released in Germany with the vocals of pop stars Max Raabe and Nina Hagen backed by the Ensemble Modern. Most recently, two revivals premiered in 2006: in New York City, a Broadway production at Studio 54, starring Alan Cummings and Cyndi Lauper, with a new adaptation by Wallace Shawn; and a production at the Berlin Admiralspalast under the direction of movie star Klaus Maria Brandauer and starring the German punk rock star Campesino.

THE PROOF OF THE PUDDING: READING *THE THREEPENNY OPERA*

The Threepenny Opera is a modern adaptation of John Gay's *The Beggar's Opera* from 1728, and much of Gay's original is still to be found in the Brecht / Weill / Hauptmann modernization. Although not included in this edition, the reader would only be enriched by perusing Gay's original. Additionally, it is highly recommended to listen to the production's soundtrack. The 1930 soundtrack gives a sense of the raw Jazz Age tension, as well as renditions of several songs sung by Brecht himself. The 1954 American soundtrack is notable for two reasons: 1) it defined much of the *Threepenny* reception for American theatergoers through the 1980s; and 2) it is a relatively tame translation of the brutal language contained in the original. Finally, one cannot overlook the tremendous cultural history of the song "Mac the Knife." Over the years nearly everyone has rendered a version, from Louis Armstrong, Bobby Darin, Frank Sinatra, Ella Fitzgerald, and Nick Cave to the 1980s McDonald's ad campaign featuring "Mac, Tonight." Understanding the ubiquity of this one song will give the reader a sense of how pervasively *The Threepenny Opera* has infiltrated our cultural landscape.

In contrast to his later works, in which he would produce accompanying theoretical notes along with the primary playscript, all the secondary notes for *The Threepenny Opera* were written after the finished version, and hence, at times, feel somewhat strained. Brecht was struggling with not only the huge commercial success of the play, which made for a tough fit with his newfound interest in Marxism, but also with a theoretical language to talk about his dramatic work. Nevertheless the short notes from Brecht, as well as from Weill, on how to present the play provide additional insight into Brecht's artistic intent and can easily be accessed during reading of the playscript. Perhaps, the most important secondary text is the transcript of the conversation between the Italian director Giorgio Strehler and Brecht in 1955, shortly before the premiere of the play in Milan. Strehler would prove to be one of the great interpreters of Brecht's work throughout the mid- to late-twentieth century, and the points brought out in this conversation will be quite useful for the reader.

NORMAN ROESSLER

Introduction

First staged only two years after *Man equals Man*, *The Three-penny Opera* was a very different kind of achievement. For where the earlier play had its roots in Brecht's Augsburg youth and developed under a variety of influences over many years, *The Threepenny Opera*—or, more precisely, Brecht's contribution to it—was quickly written for a specific purpose. Moreover although both remained among his favourite plays he showed his affection this time not by continually revising the text as he did with *Man equals Man* but by leaving the original version unchanged and instead developing it first as a film story, then as a novel. What we have here therefore is the work as it was written and staged just half a century ago in 1928. Like all his plays it is something of a montage, embracing elements from different sources and periods. But far more than most of them it remains nailed to a particular moment in German history.

The second half of the 1920s was the stable period of the Weimar Republic, starting in 1924, once the effects of the inflation began to be overcome and the new American capital began flowing into the country, and ending in 1929 with the Wall Street crash. In the theatre it began with a succession of new-style productions, among which Brecht's *Edward II* and Erich Engel's *Coriolanus* early in 1925 were significant as leading to a general re-evaluation of the classics; but the real landmark was Carl Zuckmayer's *Der fröhliche Weinberg* at the end of that year, with its revelation of the public appetite for literate but unpretentious down-to-earth comedy. Brecht at this time was trying to grapple with the problem of writing plays about the modern world, with all its economic complexities and its wide-ranging interrelationships, and this led both to a more conscious development of the 'epic' form and to a new fascination with the economic analysis put forward by Karl Marx, whom he started reading in 1926. It must have been this twofold interest, coupled with his growing reputation as one of the most vocal and original of the younger playwrights, that took him into the collective of 'dramaturgs' formed by Erwin Piscator when he set up his first independent company at the Theater am Nollendorfplatz in the autumn of 1927. Though this was a Berlin West End theatre, appealing largely to a fashionable audience, its politics were Communist and its four productions established new ways of tackling just the sort of themes that had begun plaguing Brecht. None the less the particular plays which he was trying to write—notably *Joe P. Fleischhacker*, based on Frank Norris's novel *The Pit* about the Chicago wheat market, and *Decline of the Egoist Johann Fatzer* about soldiers deserting in the First World War—were neither performed there nor even completed. Indeed from *Man equals Man* in 1926 to *Saint Joan of the Stockyards* in 1931 he remained unable to finish the large-scale plays that preoccupied him most.

At the same time his first meeting with Kurt Weill in the spring of 1927, soon after Weill's enthusiastic review of the Berlin Radio broadcast of *Man equals Man*, gave him a new and promising line to follow. Weill, who had been one of Busoni's handful of pupils at the Berlin Academy, was becoming known as a dissonant, strongly contrapuntal neo-classical composer to be ranked with Hindemith, Toch and Ernst Křenek, but he was also a man of considerable literary judgement who had been collaborating with two of the few playwrights about whom Brecht had anything good to say: Georg Kaiser and Iwan Goll. Enormously impressed not only by the broadcast but also by Brecht's first book of poems, the *Devotions*, Weill now wished to collaborate with him too. According to Weill's account they had no sooner met than they started discussing the opera medium; the word 'Mahagonny' cropped up, and with it the notion of a 'paradise city'. In other words, so it would appear, Brecht at the outset introduced him to that notion of a 'Mahagonny Opera' which he had brought with him from Munich (originally with his first wife Marianne in mind, she being an opera singer), and which related to the 'Mahagonny Songs' in the *Devotions*. The idea of turning this into a full-scale opera was thus already in the air when Weill got a commission to contribute one of a series of short operas to the forthcoming Baden-Baden 'German Chamber Music' festival that summer. Basing himself on the 'Mahagonny Songs', and making some use of Brecht's own tunes for them, he started in May to compose the jazzy 'songspiel' now known as *The Little Mahagonny* which was performed at Baden-Baden in a boxing-ring stage in July. After this the two collaborators worked throughout the rest of the year on the libretto for the full-scale opera, which was ready for Weill to begin composing early in 1928.

In effect then it can be said that Brecht started the year of *The Threepenny Opera* with three main irons in the fire. There was his technically and politically stimulating job with Piscator, which was now involving him in the rewriting of the official *Schweik* adaptation to suit the revolutionary staging which Piscator and his designer George Grosz had devised. There were his own incomplete social-political plays, one of which—*Fleischhacker*—had already been announced on Piscator's prospectus. And then there was the very promising collaboration with Weill, involving also his own preferred designer Caspar Neher (who was outside Piscator's scheme of things). Looking now at the state of the German theatre at the time it can be seen that any reliance on Piscator involved considerable risks, for he was already far exceeding his budgeted costs and the combination of bad planning and expensive technical innovations was soon to be fatal. None the less it was Piscator who sparked off a wave of interest in the *Zeitstück*, or 'play of the times', from which a number of other left-wing writers benefited and which might well have led to a production for one of Brecht's essays in the genre. Oddly enough, however, it was the opera medium which reflected this first, following the impact of Křenek's jazz opera *Jonny spielt auf* in February (Leipzig première) and October (Berlin production) 1927. And with Klemperer's appointment that year to head the Kroll-Oper, the second state opera house in Berlin, a unique centre for modern opera was created in which such associates of Brecht's as Neher and Ernst Legal and Jacob Geis (both of whom had been involved with *Man equals Man*) were soon to find employment.

––––––––

The critical moment came in March–April 1928, when Piscator had taken on a second theatre and was fast heading for bankruptcy. Some three months earlier a new management had been set up in Berlin, headed by a young actor called Ernst-Josef Aufricht, once a member of Berthold Viertel's much respected company 'Die Truppe'. Around Christmas he had been given 100,000 marks by his father with which to open his own Berlin theatre, and he used this to rent the medium-sized late nineteenth-century Theater am Schiffbauerdamm not far from Reinhardt's Deutsches Theater. He booked Erich Engel, then busy with Brecht's *Man equals Man* at the Volksbühne, to direct the opening production, if possible to coincide with his own twenty-eighth birthday on 31 August. All that remained was to find a play. This was not quite so simple, even after he had brought in a young friend of Karl Kraus's called Heinrich Fischer to help him and act as his deputy. Kraus, Wedekind, Toller, Feuchtwanger, Kaiser, even the much older Sudermann were in turn considered or actually approached, but to no effect. Then one of those happy accidents occurred which go to make theatre history: Fischer ran into Brecht in a café, introduced him to Aufricht and asked if he had anything that would answer their needs. Brecht's own work in progress—presumably *Fleischhacker*—would not do; it was already promised—presumably to Piscator—and Aufricht appears to have been bored by his account of it. But Brecht also mentioned a translation of John Gay's *The Beggar's Opera* which his collaborator Elisabeth Hauptmann had begun making the previous November. This eighteenth-century satire had been an immense success in Nigel Playfair's revival at the Lyric, Hammersmith some five or six years earlier, and to the two entrepreneurs the idea 'smelt of theatre'. They read all that had so far been written, under the provisional title *Gesindel*, or *Scum*, and decided that this was the play with which to open.

Just how much Brecht had had to do with the script at this exploratory stage is uncertain, but he now took the lead and proposed that Weill should be brought in to write modern settings for the songs. Aufricht, by his own account, thereupon went privately to hear two of Weill's Kaiser operas, was appalled by their atonality and told his musical director Theo Mackeben to get hold of the traditional Pepusch arrangements in case Weill came up with something impossibly rebarbative. In mid-May the whole team were packed off to Le Lavandou in the south of France to complete the work: the Brechts, the Weills, Hauptmann, Engel. Here, and subsequently on the Ammersee in Bavaria, Brecht seems to have written some brand-new scenes (the stable wedding for instance, which bears no relation to Gay's original), and started adding his own songs, four of them piratically derived from a German version of Villon. On 1 August rehearsals started, with a duplicated script which, as our notes show, still contained a good deal of the original work, as well as songs by Gay himself and Rudyard Kipling which later disappeared. A succession of accidents, catastrophes and stopgaps then occurred. Carola Neher, who was to play Polly, arrived a fortnight late from her husband Klabund's deathbed, and abandoned her part; Roma Bahn was recruited and learned it in four days. Feuchtwanger suggested the new title; Karl Kraus added the second verse to the Jealousy Duet. Helene Weigel, cast as Mrs Coaxer the brothel Madame, developed appendicitis and the part was cut. The cabaret singer Rosa Valetti objected to the 'Song of Sexual Obsession' which she had to sing as Mrs Peachum, so this too went; Käte Kühl as Lucy could not manage the florid solo which Weill had written for another actress in scene 8, so this was eliminated and later the scene itself was cut;

Weill's young wife Lotte Lenya was accidentally left off the
printed programme; the play was found to be three-quarters of
an hour too long, leading to massive cuts in Peachum's part and
the dropping of the 'Solomon Song'; the finale was only written
during the rehearsals; and late on the 'Ballad of Mac the Knife'
was added as an inspired after-thought.

All accounts agree that the production's prospects seemed
extremely bad, with only Weill's music and Caspar Neher's sets
remaining unaffected by the mounting chaos. Even the costumes were simply those available, so Brecht was to say later
(p. 108), while the Victorian setting was decided less by the
needs of the story than by the shortage of time. The dress rehearsal must have been disastrous, the reactions of the first-night
audience a confirmation of this, lasting right into the second
scene, even after the singing of 'Pirate Jenny' in the stable. But
with the 'Cannon Song' the applause suddenly burst loose.
Quite unexpectedly, inspiredly, improvisedly, management and
collaborators found themselves with the greatest German hit of
the 1920s on their hands.

———

It struck Berlin during an interregnum, as it were: at a moment
when Piscator had temporarily disappeared as an active force in
the left-wing theatre and the various collective groups which
succeeded him had not yet got off the ground. For Brecht and
Weill there was now the composition of *Mahagonny* to be
resumed—something that was only completed in November
1929—as well as a small Berlin Requiem which Weill had
agreed to write for Radio Frankfurt on texts by Brecht, and
which they sketched out in November and December 1928.
Both men probably also had some involvement in the production of Feuchtwanger's second 'Anglo-Saxon Play' *Die Petroleu-
minseln* at the Staatstheater in the former month, for which
Weill wrote the music and Neher once more provided sets. But
the immediate effect of *The Threepenny Opera*'s success was to
establish the Theater am Schiffbauerdamm as the leading left-
wing theatre of the moment in Berlin. Retrospectively Brecht
came to speak of it as 'his' theatre, and indeed to a great extent

he does seem to have dominated its entire opening season. For with *The Threepenny Opera* temporarily transferred to another theatre (and Carola Neher at some point assuming her original role as Polly), he took over the direction of Marieluise Fleisser's anti-militarist Bavarian farce *Die Pioniere von Ingolstadt*, a sequel to the play which he had recommended to the Junge Bühne three years earlier. This opened on 31 March 1929 and featured an unknown actor whom Brecht had advised Aufricht to engage on a three-year contract—Peter Lorre—along with Kurt Gerron and Lenya, the Brown and Jenny from his own play. The farce itself was too outspoken for the police and the military, and had to be bowdlerised, but it none the less ran for two months and broke even; Aufricht later judged it the best of all the productions which he sponsored. Then *The Threepenny Opera* returned for the rest of the season, and the problem of the next play had to be faced.

Aufricht wanted another Brecht–Weill work on the same lines as before. It was scheduled once more for 31 August; Engel and Neher were again booked, and a number of the same actors already under contract. But the moment had passed, the first symptoms of the imminent economic crisis were beginning to make themselves felt, the veneer of political tolerance was wearing thin. Brecht had a seismographic feeling for such changes, and he was already heading towards a much more didactic kind of theatre, in which he briefly also managed to involve Weill. As a result *Happy End*, the Chicago comedy which was supposed to follow up *The Threepenny Opera*'s success, never really stirred his interest or drew the same inspired ideas from him as had Gay's inherently much superior original. Superficially the prospects might have seemed the same as before, with Elisabeth Hauptmann providing the basic dialogue and Brecht writing a number of characteristic songs, some of them eliciting first-rate settings from Weill. But whereas in 1928 Brecht was willing to make many radical changes in the former, so that his stamp on the final play is unmistakable, only a year later this was no longer the case. At some point during the spring of 1929 he began writing his first *Lehrstücke* or didactic plays under the twofold influence of the Japanese Noh drama and Hindemith's concept of *Gemeinschaftsmusik*—the educational implications of making music in common. Two works for that summer's Baden-Baden festival resulted. Almost at the same time his hitherto uncommitted left-wing opinions crystallised as a consequence, it seems, of the Berlin May Day demonstration at which the police killed thirty-one people. From then on he was aligned with the German Communist Party, and if this led him to foist a more 'provocative' ending on *Happy End* it also helped further to alienate him from that play without making it appear any better in the eyes of the party critics.

But, however Brecht himself might be changing at this time, *The Threepenny Opera* was a play which he had no wish to discard. Obviously it was a very much better and solider work than its successor, though the latter's rehabilitation in the 1960s (which has led it to be performed under Brecht's name in both England and the U.S.) shows the silliness of its text to be not quite the liability it once seemed. The major difference, however, lay in the former work's enormous success, which kept it running in different parts of Germany until the Nazis took over and in other countries longer still. This did not immediately tempt Brecht to tinker with the text of the play (as he continued to do with *Man equals Man*), but when Warner Brothers and Tobis, acting through producers called Nero-Film, contracted in May 1930 to make a film version he started looking at it with changed—and changing—eyes. Though sound film was then in its infancy, the prospects seemed good: G. W. Pabst was to be the director, Lania (of Piscator's old collective) to write the script; Carola Neher would play Polly, Lenya Jenny; while Brecht and Weill were given a say respectively in the script and the music. Two parallel versions would be made, one German and one French. That summer, accordingly, Brecht wrote Lania the treatment called 'Die Beule', 'The Bruise', which in effect ignores all that had remained of *The Beggar's Opera* and uses the characters and the Victorian London setting to point a radically changed moral. Everything now is on a larger scale—the gang is 120 strong, Peachum heads a Begging Trust—and a higher social level, with peers, a general and a magistrate at Macheath's wedding in the ducal manège. The gang and the beggars this time are engaged in a war whose symbol is the bruise inflicted by the former on a beggar called Sam. Peachum accordingly uses the beggars to disfigure the smartly repainted slum streets through which the Queen is to pass; he interviews Brown with seven lawyers behind him, and secures Macheath's arrest after a bucolic picnic and a chase in which a car full of policemen pursues a car full of whores. There is no escape and no second arrest. Under Polly's direction the gang has simply taken over the National Deposit Bank and converted itself into a group of solemn financiers. Both they and Mrs Peachum now become uneasy about the dangers of unleashing the poor; while Brown has a terrible dream, in which thousands of poor people emerge from under one of the Thames bridges as a great flood, sweeping through the streets and public buildings. So the 'mounted Messengers' this time are the bankers who arrive to bail Macheath out; and rather than disappoint the crowds Peachum hands over Sam to be hanged instead. The social façades are maintained as Macheath joins the reunited bourgeoisie awaiting the arrival of their Queen.

This scheme, on which Neher and the Bulgarian director Slatan Dudow also collaborated, was plainly unwelcome to the producers, and the fact that Brecht only met the agreed August deadline by communicating it to Lania orally did not improve matters. Though Lania needed him to continue working, the Nero firm chose to dismiss Brecht at this stage, and brought in the Communist film critic Béla Balázs to help complete the script. A law suit followed, which Brecht lost, and thereafter he had no words too bad for Pabst's film, which meanwhile went obstinately ahead, to be shown in Berlin on 19 February 1931. Though the long theoretical essay which Brecht thereafter wrote on the 'Threepenny Lawsuit', as he termed it, is an illuminating work, not least for its links with the ideas of his new friend Walter Benjamin, the modern reader should not allow its downright condemnation to put him off the film. For in fact not only did the latter capture aspects of the original (for instance

Carola Neher's interpretation of Polly) that necessarily elude any modern production, but it also incorporates a surprising proportion of Brecht's changes to the story. These, however, continued to itch Brecht, so that while leaving the play itself as it had been in the 1928 production (with all its last-minute decisions and improvisations) he was soon planning its further development in *The Threepenny Novel*, his one substantial work of fiction, which he was to hand in to its Dutch publisher some months after leaving Germany in 1933. Engel, when he came again to direct the play at the Theater am Schiffbauerdamm for the Berliner Ensemble in 1960, after Brecht's death, wondered at first if he could not incorporate some of the ideas from 'The Bruise' and the novel, but soon decided that they were too divergent from the play. Brecht for his part wrote some topical versions of the songs (p. 87 ff.) for other directors in the immediate post-war years, but it is not clear if and when they were used, and certainly he never made them a permanent part of the text; indeed they hardly merit it. All the same, his discussions in connection with Giorgio Strehler's Milan production in the last year of his life (p. 105) show that he regarded *The Threepenny Opera* as no inviolable museum piece. For he envisaged a new framework, and welcomed Strehler's updating of the story to the era of the Keystone Cops.

———

Like *Man equals Man, The Threepenny Opera* presents a problem to earnest-minded interpreters, since it is hard to reconcile its flippancies with Brecht's status as a Communist playwright, while its repeated successes in the commercial theatres of bourgeois society—from Berlin of the 1920s to New York of the 1970s—take some explaining away. The trouble here is not only that when Brecht actually wrote his share of this play he was only beginning to explore Marxism and had barely begun to relate to the class struggle (as the leading Communist Party critic Alfred Kemény pointed out), but that the issue was subsequently confused by Brecht's writing all his own notes and interpretations *after* adopting a more committed position in 1929. His remarks moreover are too easily taken out of context and at their face value: his insistence, for instance, that the play is a critique of bourgeois society and not merely of the *Lumpenproletariat* was only a retort—quite unsubstantiated—to that ill-disposed critic in the party's daily *Die Rote Fahne* who had accused him of the contrary, referred to him as 'the Bohemian Bert Brecht' and dismissed the whole work as a money-spinner containing 'Not a vestige of modern social or political satire'. Just like Piscator's productions of the previous season *The Threepenny Opera* undoubtedly appealed to the fashionable Berlin public and subsequently to the middle classes throughout Germany, and if it gave them an increasingly cynical view of their own institutions it does not seem to have prompted either them or any other section of society to try to change these for the better. The fact was simply that 'one has to have seen it', as the elegant and cosmopolitan Count Kessler noted in his diary after doing so with a party that included an ambassador and a director of the Dresdner Bank.

Brecht himself had far too much affection for this work to admit the ineffectiveness of its message, even after he had tacitly confirmed such accusations by going over to austerer, explicitly didactic forms. Even years later he could still view it through something of a pink cloud, as indicated by his wishful replies to Giorgio Strehler on p. 107. Yet the most favourable criticisms at the time were concerned less with its attack on 'bourgeois morality' and capitalist property rights as being based on theft than with its establishment of a highly original new theatrical genre. Thus Herbert Ihering, who from the first had been Brecht's leading supporter among the Berlin critics, while welcoming this 'new form, open to every possibility, every kind of content', pointed out that 'this content, however, has still to come'. Part of the common over-estimation of the play's social purpose and impact is due most probably to the intense dislike felt for it by the German nationalist reaction which began gaining ground within a year of the première and was soon to bring the Nazis their first great electoral successes. It was a time of growing polarisation in German political and cultural life, and if the Berlin theatre continued to move leftwards, dragging part of the cinema with it, there was now much less hesitation on the part of the authorities and the great middlebrow public to voice their dislike of anything 'alien' and 'decadent' in the arts. Not only was Weill a leading target for such campaigns, largely on racialist grounds, but the brothel scene and the cynicism of the songs were certainly enough to qualify Brecht too, whether or not he represented any kind of serious threat. A great wave of irrational feeling was building up, and in so far as it was directed against *The Threepenny Opera* its political aspects were quite deceptive. Thus that shrewd observer Kurt Tucholsky could write in spring 1930 that the battle was a sham one because the work itself was unrealistic. 'This writer can be compared to a man cooking soup on a burning house. It isn't he who caused the fire.'

Yet if its political significance is often overrated today *The Threepenny Opera* remains revolutionary in a less obvious but equally disturbing sense. For, like *The Little Mahagonny* before it, it struck almost instinctively at the whole hierarchical order of the arts, with opera on its Wagnerian pinnacle at the top, and reshuffled highbrow and lowbrow elements to form a new kind of musical theatre which would upset every accepted notion of what was socially and culturally proper. This was what the best critics immediately recognised, Ihering writing that the success of *The Threepenny Opera* was of immense importance:

> A theatre that is not smart, not geared to 'society', has broken through to the audience.

Far more so the musicians; thus Klemperer included the wind suite from the music in his concerts and is reported to have seen the 1928 production ten times, while Heinrich Strobel compared it with *The Soldier's Tale* as 'showing the way' and Theodor Adorno judged it the most important event since Berg's *Wozzeck*. In many ways the change of values which it implied has proved harder for later societies to assimilate than have the somewhat random gibes at business, religious hypocrisy, individual charity, romantic marriage and the judicial system which make up the political content of the text. Particularly when seen in conjunction with Brecht's and Walter Benjamin's current thinking about the 'apparatus' of the arts, it suggested a complete cultural and sociological re-evaluation which would alter all the existing categories, starting with those of opera and operetta (for it was neither), as well as the corresponding techniques of acting, singing and so forth. Today, though certainly poverty, slums, corrupt business practices and biassed justice continue to exist in our most prosperous societies, we no longer feel that *The Threepenny Opera* has anything all that acute to say about them. But the implications of the new form for singers, musicians, voice teachers and above all for institutionalised opera are still far from fully digested. And because Brecht and his friends did not yet manage to capture the 'apparatus' of which they spoke this holds good for Communist as well as for capitalist society.

———

In reading Brecht's notes which we print it must be remembered that they were written some two years after the permière and only published in 1931. Important as they remain for the development of his theory and practice of theatre, as a guide to the interpretation of the play they tend to ignore the largely irresponsible lightheartedness with which the collaborators originally set to work. Nor is there any material in our own account of the text's evolution for those directors who would like to sharpen its attack on capitalist morality and institutions—by adding, for instance, episodes from Macheath's subsequent career as a banker in line with Brecht's film treatment in 'The Bruise'; for Brecht himself wrote no such scene. The reallocation of Polly's 'Pirate Jenny' song, too, to Jenny as in the film (where it somewhat overloads the brothel episode), is nowhere suggested by Brecht, though many directors have opted for it either to avoid the confusion of names or to build up the whore's part. What does emerge from the early scripts (of which nothing has yet been published in Germany itself) is a number of excellent passages and episodes, some of which could certainly help to clarify the story. The poisoning episode with Lucy in Act 3 is dispensable, though it came from Gay and inspired a splendid piece of musical parody from Weill, now in the miniature score. But Peachum's original conclusion to Act 2 is not only funnier than the rather laboured 'Semiramis' speech of the final version; it also explains the otherwise rather baffling start to Act 3. Similarly Lucy's disclosure of her father's drunkenness (p. 121) makes his startling ineptitude at that point easier to accept. All such passages, however, date from before 31 August 1928 and are in no sense afterthoughts or amendments in the light of Brecht's changing interpretations of his story, characters and setting. Aside from the postwar versions of some of the songs (which were not used in the Berliner Ensemble production) he left it as a play of that time.

Of course this is not going to stop directors and dramaturgs from making their own attempts to bring it up to date or put it in some framework more intelligible to a particular audience. But they must be clear that they do this on their own responsibility. They cannot claim to be doing Brecht's work for him and giving us the play 'he would have written' supposing he had been a few years older and a rather better Marxist. After all, he could perfectly well have done this himself if he had wished. Instead he allowed it to remain as it was: the occasional work of a thirty-year-old writer and a composer of twenty-eight. Central as it was to his success in the theatre, it was not in the main line of his aims and concerns either before and after. It was, and is, a brilliant but by no means flawless distraction.

THE EDITORS

The Threepenny Opera

Collaborators: ELISABETH HAUPTMANN, KURT WEILL

Translators: RALPH MANHEIM, JOHN WILLETT

Characters
MACHEATH, *called Mac the Knife*
JONATHAN JEREMIAH PEACHUM, *proprietor of the Beggar's Friend Ltd*
CELIA PEACHUM, *his wife*
POLLY PEACHUM, *his daughter*
BROWN, *High Sheriff of London*
LUCY, *his daughter*
LOW-DIVE JENNY
SMITH
THE REVEREND KIMBALL
FILCH
A BALLAD SINGER
THE GANG
Beggars
Whores
Constables

PROLOGUE

THE BALLAD OF MAC THE KNIFE

Fair in Soho.

The beggars are begging, the thieves are stealing, the whores are whoring. A ballad singer sings a ballad.

See the shark with teeth like razors.
All can read his open face.
And Macheath has got a knife, but
Not in such an obvious place.

See the shark, how red his fins are
As he slashes at his prey.
Mac the Knife wears white kid gloves which
Give the minimum away.

By the Thames's turbid waters
Men abruptly tumble down.
Is it plague or is it cholera?
Or a sign Macheath's in town?

On a beautiful blue Sunday
See a corpse stretched in the Strand.
See a man dodge round the corner . . .
Mackie's friends will understand.

And Schmul Meier, reported missing
Like so many wealthy men:
Mac the Knife acquired his cash box.
God alone knows how or when.

Peachum goes walking across the stage from left to right with his wife and daughter.

> Jenny Towler turned up lately
> With a knife stuck through her breast
> While Macheath walks the Embankment
> Nonchalantly unimpressed.
>
> Where is Alfred Gleet the cabman?
> Who can get that story clear?
> All the world may know the answer
> Just Macheath has no idea.
>
> And the ghastly fire in Soho—
> Seven children at a go—
> In the crowd stands Mac the Knife, but he
> Isn't asked and doesn't know.
>
> And the child-bride in her nightie
> Whose assailant's still at large
> Violated in her slumbers—
> Mackie, how much did you charge?

Laughter among the whores. A man steps out from their midst and walks quickly away across the square.

LOW-DIVE JENNY: That was Mac the Knife!

ACT ONE

I

TO COMBAT THE INCREASING CALLOUSNESS OF MANKIND, J. PEACHUM, A MAN OF BUSINESS, HAS OPENED A SHOP WHERE THE POOREST OF THE POOR CAN ACQUIRE AN EXTERIOR THAT WILL TOUCH THE HARDEST OF HEARTS.

Jonathan Jeremiah Peacham's outfitting shop for beggars.

PEACHUM'S MORNING HYMN

You ramshackle Christian, awake!
Get on with your sinful employment
Show what a good crook you could make.
The Lord will cut short your enjoyment.

Betray your own brother, you rogue
And sell your old woman, you rat.
You think the Lord God's just a joke?
He'll give you His Judgement on that.

PEACHUM *to the audience:* Something new is needed. My business is too hard, for my business is arousing human sympathy. There are a few things that stir men's souls, just a few, but the trouble is that after repeated use they lose their effect. Because man has the abominable gift of being able to deaden his feelings as well, so to speak. Suppose, for instance, a man sees another man standing on the corner with a stump for an arm; the first time he may be shocked enough to give him tenpence, but the second time it will only be fivepence, and if he sees him a third time he'll hand him over to the police without batting an eyelash. It's the same with the spiritual approach. *A large sign saying 'It is more blessed to give than to receive' is lowered from the grid.* What good are the most beautiful, the most poignant sayings, painted on the most enticing little signs, when they get expended so quickly? The Bible has four or five sayings that stir the heart; once a man has expended them, there's nothing for it but starvation. Take this one, for instance—'Give and it shall be given unto you'—how threadbare it is after hanging here a mere three weeks. Yes, you have to keep on offering something new. So it's back to the good old Bible again, but how long can it go on providing?

Knocking. Peachum opens. Enter a young man by the name of Filch.

FILCH: Messrs Peachum & Co.?

PEACHUM: Peachum.

FILCH: Are you the proprietor of The Beggar's Friend Ltd.? I've been sent to you. Fine slogans you've got there! Money in the bank, those are. Got a whole library full of them, I suppose? That's what I call really something. What chance has a bloke like me got to think up ideas like that; and how can business progress without education?

PEACHUM: What's your name?

FILCH: It's this way, Mr Peachum, I've been down on my luck since a boy. Mother drank, father gambled. Left to my own resources at an early age, without a mother's tender hand, I sank deeper and deeper into the quicksands of the big city. I've never known a father's care or the blessings of a happy home. So now you see me . . .

PEACHUM: So now I see you . . .

FILCH *confused:* . . . bereft of all support, a prey to my baser instincts.

PEACHUM: Like a derelict on the high seas and so on. Now tell me, derelict, which district have you been reciting that fairy story in?

FILCH: What do you mean, Mr Peachum?

PEACHUM: You deliver that speech in public, I take it?

FILCH: Well, it's this way, Mr Peachum, yesterday there was an unpleasant little incident in Highland Street. There I am, standing on the corner quiet and miserable, holding out my hat, no suspicion of anything nasty . . .

PEACHUM *leafs through a notebook:* Highland Street. Yes, yes, right. You're the bastard that Honey and Sam caught yesterday. You had the impudence to be molesting passers-by in District 10. We let you off with a thrashing because we had reason to believe you didn't know what's what. But if you show your face again it'll be the chop for you. Got it?

FILCH: Please, Mr Peachum, please. What can I do, Mr Peachum? The gentlemen beat me black and blue and then they gave me your business card. If I took off my coat, you'd think you were looking at a fish on a slab.

PEACHUM: My friend, if you're not flat as a kipper, then my men weren't doing their job properly. Along come these young whipper-snappers who think they've only got to hold out their paw to land a steak. What would you say if some-one started fishing the best trout out of your pond?

FILCH: It's like this, Mr Peachum—I haven't got a pond.

PEACHUM: Licences are delivered to professionals only. *Points in a businesslike way to a map of the city.* London is divided into fourteen districts. Any man who intends to practise the craft of begging in any one of them needs a licence from Jonathan Jeremiah Peachum & Co. Why, anybody could come along—a prey to his baser instincts.

FILCH: Mr Peachum, only a few shillings stand between me and utter ruin. Something must be done. With two shillings in my pocket I . . .

PEACHUM: One pound.

FILCH: Mr Peachum!

Points imploringly at a sign saying 'Do not turn a deaf ear to misery!' Peachum points to the curtain over a showcase, on which is written: 'Give and it shall be given unto you!'

FILCH: Ten bob.

PEACHUM: Plus fifty per cent of your take, settle up once a week. With outfit seventy per cent.

FILCH: What does the outfit consist of?

PEACHUM: That's for the firm to decide.

FILCH: Which district could I start in?

PEACHUM: Baker Street. Numbers 2 to 104. That comes even cheaper. Only fifty per cent, including the outfit.

FILCH: Very well. *He pays.*

PEACHUM: Your name?

FILCH: Charles Filch.

PEACHUM: Right. *Shouts.* Mrs Peachum! *Mrs Peachum enters.* This is Filch. Number 314. Baker Street district. I'll do his entry myself. Trust you to pick this moment to apply, just before the Coronation, when for once in a lifetime there's a chance of making a little something. Outfit C. *He opens a linen curtain before a showcase in which there are five wax dummies.*

FILCH: What's that?

PEACHUM: Those are the five basic types of misery, those most likely to touch the human heart. The sight of such types puts a man into the unnatural state where he is willing to part with money. Outfit A: Victim of vehicular progress. The merry paraplegic, always cheerful—*He acts it out.*—always carefree, emphasised by arm-stump. Outfit B: Victim of the Higher Strategy. The Tiresome Trembler, molests passers-by, operates by inspiring nausea—*He acts it out.*—attenuated by medals. Outfit C: Victim of advanced Technology. The Pitiful Blind Man, the Cordon Bleu of Beggary.

He acts it out, staggering toward Filch. The moment he bumps into Filch, Filch cries out in horror. Peachum stops at once, looks at him with amazement and suddenly roars.

He's *sorry* for me! You'll never be a beggar as long as you live! You're only fit to be begged from! Very well, outfit D!

Celia, you've been drinking again. And now you can't see straight. Number 136 has complained about his outfit. How often do I have to tell you that a gentleman doesn't put on filthy clothes? The only thing about it that could inspire pity was the stains and they should have been added by just ironing in candle wax. Use your head! Have I got to do everything myself? *To Filch:* Take off your clothes and put this on, but mind you, look after it!

FILCH: What about my things?

PEACHUM: Property of the firm. Outfit E: young man who has seen better days or, if you'd rather, never thought it would come to this.

FILCH: Oh, you use them again? Why can't *I* do the better days act?

PEACHUM: Because nobody can make his own suffering sound convincing, my boy. If you have a bellyache and say so, people will simply be disgusted. Anyway, you're not here to ask questions but to put these things on.

FILCH: Aren't they rather dirty? *After Peachum has given him a penetrating look.* Excuse me, sir, please excuse me.

MRS PEACHUM: Shake a leg, son, I'm not standing here holding your trousers till Christmas.

FILCH: *suddenly emphatic:* But I'm not taking my shoes off! Absolutely not. I'd sooner pack the whole thing in. They're the only present my poor mother ever gave me, I may have sunk pretty low, but never . . .

MRS PEACHUM: Stop driveling. We all know your feet are dirty.

FILCH: Where am I supposed to wash my feet? In midwinter? *Mrs Peachum leads him behind a screen, then she sits down on the left and starts ironing candle wax into a suit.*

PEACHUM: Where's your daughter?

MRS PEACHUM: Polly? Upstairs.

PEACHUM: Has that man been here again? The one who's always coming round when I'm out?

MRS PEACHUM: Don't be so suspicious, Jonathan, there's no finer gentleman. The Captain takes a real interest in our Polly.

PEACHUM: I see.

MRS PEACHUM: And if I've got half an eye in my head, Polly thinks he's very nice too.

PEACHUM: Celia, the way you chuck your daughter around anyone would think I was a millionaire. Wanting to marry her off? The idea! Do you think this lousy business of ours would survive a week if those ragamuffins our customers had nothing better than *our* legs to look at? A husband! He'd have us in his clutches in three shakes! In his clutches! Do you think your daughter can hold her tongue in bed any better than you?

MRS PEACHUM: A fine opinion of your daughter you have.

PEACHUM: The worst. The very worst. A lump of sensuality, that's what she is.

MRS PEACHUM: If so, she didn't get it from you.

PEACHUM: Marriage! I expect my daughter to be to me as bread to the hungry. *He leafs in the Book.* It even says so in the Bible somewhere. Anyway marriage is disgusting. I'll teach her to get married.

MRS PEACHUM: Jonathan, you're just a barbarian.

PEACHUM: Barbarian! What's this gentleman's name?

MRS PEACHUM: They never call him anything but 'the Captain'.

PEACHUM: So you haven't even asked him his name? Interesting.

MRS PEACHUM: You don't suppose we'd ask for a birth certificate when such a distinguished gentleman invites Polly and me to the Cuttlefish Hotel for a little hop.

PEACHUM: Where?

MRS PEACHUM: To the Cuttlefish Hotel for a little hop.

PEACHUM: Captain? Cuttlefish Hotel? Hm, hm, hm . . .

MRS PEACHUM: A gentleman who has always handled me and my daughter with kid gloves.

PEACHUM: Kid gloves!

MRS PEACHUM: Honest, he always does wear gloves, white ones: white kid gloves.

PEACHUM: I see. White gloves and a cane with an ivory handle and spats and patent-leather shoes and a charismatic personality and a scar . . .

MRS PEACHUM: On his neck. Isn't there anyone you don't know? *Filch crawls out from behind the screen.*

FILCH: Mr Peachum, couldn't you give me a few tips, I've always believed in having a system and not just shooting off my mouth any old how.

MRS PEACHUM: A system!

PEACHUM: He can be a half-wit. Come back this evening at six, we'll teach you the rudiments. Now piss off!

FILCH: Thank you very much indeed, Mr Peachum. Many thanks. *Goes out.*

PEACHUM: Fifty per cent!—And now I'll tell you who this gentleman with the gloves is—Mac the Knife! *He runs up the stairs to Polly's bedroom.*

MRS PEACHUM: God in Heaven! Mac the Knife! Jesus! Gentle Jesus meek and mild—Polly! Where's Polly?
Peachum comes down slowly.

PEACHUM: Polly? Polly's not come home. Her bed has not been slept in.

MRS PEACHUM: She'll have gone to supper with that wool merchant. That'll be it, Jonathan.

PEACHUM: Let's hope to God it is the wool merchant!
Mr and Mrs Peachum step before the curtain and sing. Song lighting: golden glow. The organ is lit up. Three lamps are lowered from above on a pole, and the signs say:

THE 'NO THEY CAN'T' SONG

No, they can't
Bear to be at home all tucked up tight in bed.
It's fun they want
You can bet they've got some fancy notions brewing up instead.

So that's your Moon over Soho
That is your infernal 'd'you feel my heart beating?' line.
That's the old 'wherever you go I shall be with you, honey'
When you first fall in love and the moonbeams shine.

No, they can't
See what's good for them and set their mind on it.

It's fun they want
So they end up on their arses in the shit.

Then where's your Moon over Soho?
What's come of your infernal 'd'you feel my heart beating?' bit?
Where's the old 'wherever you go I shall be with you, honey'?
When you're no more in love, and you're in the shit?

2

DEEP IN THE HEART OF SOHO THE BANDIT MAC THE
KNIFE IS CELEBRATING HIS MARRIAGE TO POLLY
PEACHUM, THE BEGGAR KING'S DAUGHTER.

Bare Stable.

MATTHEW, *known as Matt of the Mint, holds out his revolver
and searches the stable with a lantern:* Hey, hands up, any-
body that's here!
*Macheath enters and makes a tour of inspection along the
foot-lights.*
MACHEATH: Well, is there anybody?
MATTHEW: Not a soul. Just the place for our wedding.
POLLY *enters in wedding dress:* But it's a stable!
MAC: Sit on the feed-bin for the moment, Polly. *To the audi-
ence:* Today this stable will witness my marriage to Miss
Polly Peachum, who has followed me for love in order to
share my life with me.
MATTHEW: All over London they'll be saying this is the most
daring job you've ever pulled, Mac, enticing Mr Peachum's
only child from his home.
MAC: Who's Mr Peachum?
MATTHEW: He'll tell you he's the poorest man in London.
POLLY: But you can't be meaning to have our wedding here?
Why, it is a common stable. You can't ask the vicar to a place
like this. Besides, it isn't even ours. We really oughtn't to start

our new life with a burglary, Mac. Why, this is the biggest day of our life.

MAC: Dear child, everything shall be done as you wish. We can't have you embarrassed in any way. The trimmings will be here in a moment.

MATTHEW: That'll be the furniture.

Large vans are heard driving up. Half a dozen men come in, carrying carpets, furniture, dishes, etc., with which they transform the stable into an exaggeratedly luxurious room.[1]*

MAC: Junk.

The gentlemen put their presents down left, congratulate the bride and report to the bridegroom.[2]

JAKE *known as Crook-fingered Jake*: Congratulations! At 14 Ginger Street there were some people on the second floor. We had to smoke them out.

BOB *known as Bob the Saw*: Congratulations! A copper got done in the Strand.

MAC: Amateurs.

NED: We did all we could, but three people in the West End were past saving. Congratulations!

MAC: Amateurs and bunglers.

JIMMY: An old gent got hurt a bit, but I don't think it's anything serious. Congratulations.

MAC: My orders were: avoid bloodshed. It makes me sick to think of it. You'll never make business men! Cannibals, perhaps, but not business men!

WALTER *known as Dreary Walt*: Congratulations. Only half an hour ago, Madam, that harpsichord belonged to the Duchess of Somerset.

POLLY: What is this furniture anyway?

MAC: How do you like the furniture, Polly?

POLLY *in tears*: Those poor people, all for a few sticks of furniture.

---

*These numbers refer to the 'Hints for actors' in the Notes p. 95 ff.

MAC: And what furniture! Junk! You have a perfect right to be angry. A rosewood harpsichord along with a renaissance sofa. That's unforgivable. What about a table?

WALTER: A table?

They lay some planks over the bins.

POLLY: Oh, Mac, I'm so miserable! I only hope the vicar doesn't come.

MATTHEW: Of course he'll come. We gave him exact directions.

WALTER *introduces the table:* A table!

MAC *seeing Polly in tears:* My wife is very much upset. Where are the rest of the chairs? A harpsichord and the happy couple has to sit on the floor! Use your heads! For once I'm having a wedding, and how often does that happen? Shut up, Dreary! And how often does it happen that I leave you to do something on your own? And when I do you start by upsetting my wife.

NED: Dear Polly . . .

MAC *knocks his hat off his head*[3]: 'Dear Polly'! I'll bash your head through your kidneys with your 'dear Polly', you squirt. Have you ever heard the like? 'Dear Polly!' I suppose you've been to bed with her?

POLLY: Mac!

NED: I swear . . .

WALTER: Dear madam, if any items of furniture should be lacking, we'll be only too glad to go back and . . .

MAC: A rosewood harpsichord and no chairs. *Laughs.* Speaking as a bride, what do you say to that?

POLLY: It could be worse.

MAC: Two chairs and a sofa and the bridal couple has to sit on the floor.

POLLY: Something new, I'd say.

MAC *sharply:* Get the legs sawn off this harpsichord! Go on!

FOUR MEN *saw the legs off the harpsichord and sing:*

Bill Lawgen and Mary Syer
Were made man and wife a week ago.

When it was over and they exchanged a kiss
He was thinking 'Whose wedding dress was this?'
While his name was one thing she'd rather like to know.
Hooray!

WALTER: The finished article, madam: there's your bench.

MAC: May I now ask the gentlemen to take off those filthy rags and put on some decent clothes? This isn't just anybody's wedding, you know. Polly, may I ask you to look after the fodder?

POLLY: Is this our wedding feast? Was the whole lot stolen, Mac?

MAC: Of course. Of course.

POLLY: I wonder what you will do if there's a knock at the door and the sheriff steps in.

MAC: I'll show you what your husband will do in that situation.

MATTHEW: It couldn't happen today. The mounted police are all sure to be in Daventry. They'll be escorting the Queen back to town for Friday's Coronation.

POLLY: Two knives and fourteen forks! One knife per chair.

MAC: What incompetence! That's the work of apprentices, not experienced men! Haven't you any sense of style? Fancy not knowing the difference between Chippendale and Louis Quatorze.

The gang comes back. The gentlemen are now wearing fashionable evening dress, but unfortunately their movements are not in keeping with it.

WALTER: We only wanted to bring the most valuable stuff. Look at that wood! Really first class.

MATTHEW: Ssst! Ssst! Permit us, Captain . . .

MAC: Polly, come here a minute.

Mac and Polly assume the pose of a couple prepared to receive congratulations.

MATTHEW: Permit us, Captain, on the greatest day of your life, in the full bloom of your career, or rather the turning point, to offer you our heartiest and at the same time most sincere congratulations, etcetera. That posh talk don't half make me

sick. So to cut a long story short—*Shakes Mac's hand.*—keep
up the good work, old mate.

MAC: Thank you, that was kind of you, Matthew.

MATTHEW *shaking Polly's hand after embracing Mac with
emotion:* It was spoken from the heart, all right! So as I was
saying, keep it up, old china, I mean—*Grinning*—the good
work of course.

*Roars of laughter from the guests. Suddenly Mac with a deft
movement sends Matthew to the floor.*

MAC: Shut your trap. Keep that filth for Kitty, she's the kind of
slut that appreciates it.

POLLY: Mac, don't be so vulgar.

MATTHEW: Here, I don't like that. Calling Kitty a slut . . .
Stands up with difficulty.

MAC: Oh, so you don't like that?

MATTHEW: And besides, I never use filthy language with her. I
respect Kitty too much. But maybe you wouldn't understand
that, the way you are. You're a fine one to talk about filth. Do
you think Lucy didn't tell me the things you've told her?
Compared to that, I'm driven snow.
Mac looks at him.

JAKE: Cut it out, this is a wedding. *They pull him away.*

MAC: Fine wedding, isn't it, Polly? Having to see trash like this
around you on the day of your marriage. You wouldn't have
thought your husband's friends would let him down. Think
about it.

POLLY: I think it's nice.

ROBERT: Blarney. Nobody's letting you down. What's a difference of opinion between friends? Kitty's as good as the next
girl. But now bring out your wedding present, mate.

ALL: Yes, hand it over!

MATTHEW *offended:* Here.

POLLY: Oh, a wedding present. How kind of you, Mr Matt of
the Mint. Look, Mac, what a lovely nightgown.

MATTHEW: Another bit of filth, eh, Captain?

MAC: Forget it. I didn't mean to hurt your feelings on this festive occasion.

WALTER: What do you say to this? Chippendale!

He unveils an enormous Chippendale grandfather clock.

MAC: Quatorze.

POLLY: It's wonderful. I'm so happy. Words fail me. You're so unbelievably kind. Oh, Mac, isn't it a shame we've no flat to put it in?

MAC: Hm, it's a start in the right direction. The great thing is to get started. Thank you kindly, Walter. Go on, clear the stuff away now. Food!

JAKE *while the others start setting the table:* Trust me to come empty-handed again. *Intensely to Polly:* Believe me, young lady, I find it most distressing.

POLLY: It doesn't matter in the least, Mr Crook-finger Jake.

JAKE: Here are the boys flinging presents right and left, and me standing here like a fool. What a situation to be in! It's always the way with me. Situations! It's enough to make your hair stand on end. The other day I meet Low-Dive Jenny; well, I say, you old cow . . .

Suddenly he sees Mac standing behind him and goes off without a word.

MAC *leads Polly to her place:* This is the best food you'll taste today, Polly. Gentlemen!

All sit down to the wedding feast.[4]

NED *indicating the china:* Beautiful dishes. Savoy Hotel.

JAKE: The plover's eggs are from Selfridge's. There was supposed to be a bucket of foie gras. But Jimmy ate it on the way, he was mad because it had a hole in it.

WALTER: We don't talk about holes in polite society.

JIMMY: Don't bolt your eggs like that, Ned, not on a day like this.

MAC: Couldn't somebody sing something? Something splendiferous?

MATTHEW *choking with laughter:* Something splendiferous? That's a first-class word. *He sits down in embarrassment under Mac's withering glance.*

MAC *knocks a bowl out of someone's hand:* I didn't mean us to start eating yet. Instead of seeing you people wade straight into the trough, I would have liked something from the heart. That's what other people do on this sort of occasion.

JAKE: What, for instance?

MAC: Am I supposed to think of everything myself? I'm not asking you to put on an opera. But you might have arranged for something else besides stuffing your bellies and making filthy jokes. Oh well, it's a day like this that you find out who your friends are.

POLLY: The salmon is marvellous, Mac.

NED: I bet you've never eaten anything like it. You get that every day at Mac the Knife's. You've landed in the honey pot all right. That's what I've always said: Mac is the right match for a girl with a feeling for higher things. As I was saying to Lucy only yesterday.

POLLY: Lucy? Mac, who is Lucy?

JAKE *embarrassed:* Lucy? Oh, nothing serious, you know. *Matthew has risen; standing behind Polly, he is waving his arms to shut Jake up.*

POLLY *sees him:* Do you want something? Salt perhaps . . . ? What were you saying, Mr Jake?

JAKE: Oh, nothing, nothing at all. The main thing I wanted to say really was nothing at all. I'm always putting my foot in it.

MAC: What have you got in your hand, Jake?

JAKE: A knife, Boss.

MAC: And what have you got on your plate?

JAKE: A trout, Boss.

MAC: I see. And with the knife you are eating the trout, are you not? It's incredible. Did you ever see the like of it, Polly? Eating his fish with a knife! Anybody who does that is just a plain swine, do you get me, Jake? Think about it. You'll have your hands full, Polly, trying to turn trash like this into a human being. Have you boys got the least idea what that is?

WALTER: A human being or a human pee-ing?

POLLY: Really, Mr Walter!

MAC: So you won't sing a song, something to brighten up the

day? Has it got to be a miserable gloomy day like any other?
And come to think of it, is anybody guarding the door? I suppose you want me to attend to that myself too? Do you want
me on this day of days to guard the door so you lot can stuff
your bellies at my expense?

WALTER *sullenly:* What do you mean at your expense?

JIMMY: Stow it, Walter boy. I'm on my way. Who's going to
come here anyway? *Goes out.*

JAKE: A fine joke on a day like this if all the wedding guests
were pulled in.

JIMMY *rushes in:* Hey, Captain. The cops!

WALTER: Tiger Brown!

MATTHEW: Nonsense, it's the Reverend Kimball.

Kimball enters.

ALL *roar:* Good evening, Reverend Kimball!

KIMBALL: So I've found you after all. I find you in a lowly hut,
a humble place but your own.

MAC: Property of the Duke of Devonshire.

POLLY: Good evening, Reverend. Oh, I'm so glad that on the
happiest day of our life you . . .

MAC: And now I request a rousing song for the Reverend Kimball.

MATTHEW: How about Bill Lawgen and Mary Syer?

JAKE: Good. Bill Lawgen might be just the thing.

KIMBALL: Be nice if you'd do a little number, boys.

MATTHEW: Let's have it, gentlemen.

*Three men rise and sing hesitantly, weakly and uncer-
tainly:*

WEDDING SONG FOR THE LESS WELL-OFF

Bill Lawgen and Mary Syer
Were made man and wife a week ago
(Three cheers for the happy couple: hip, hip, hooray!)
When it was over and they exchanged a kiss
He was thinking 'Whose wedding dress was this?'

While his name was one thing she'd rather like to know.
Hooray!

Do you know what your wife's up to? No!
Do you like her sleeping round like that? No!
Three cheers for the happy couple: Hip, hip, hooray!
Billy Lawgen told me recently
Just one part of her will do for me.
The swine.
Hooray!

MAC: Is that all? Penurious!

MATTHEW *chokes again*: Penurious is the word, gentlemen.

MAC: Shut your trap!

MATTHEW: Oh, I only meant no gusto, no fire, and so on.

POLLY: Gentlemen, if none of you wishes to perform, I myself
will sing a little song; it's an imitation of a girl I saw once in
some twopenny-halfpenny dive in Soho. She was washing
the glasses, and everybody was laughing at her, and then she
turned to the guests and said things like the things I'm going
to sing to you. Right. This is a little bar, I want you to think
of it as filthy. She stood behind it morning and night. This is
the bucket and this is the rag she washed the glasses with.
Where you are sitting, the customers were sitting laughing at
her. You can laugh too, to make it exactly the same; but if
you don't want to, you don't have to. *She starts pretending
to wash glasses, muttering to herself.* Now, for instance, one
of them—it might be you—*Pointing at Walter*—says: Well,
when's your ship coming in, Jenny?

WALTER: Well, when's your ship coming in, Jenny?

POLLY: And another says—you, for instance: Still washing up
glasses, Jenny the pirate's bride?

MATTHEW: Still washing up glasses, Jenny the pirate's bride?

POLLY: Good. And now I'll begin.

*Song lighting: golden glow. The organ is lit up. Three lamps
are lowered from above on a pole, and the signs say:*

PIRATE JENNY

Now you gents all see I've the glasses to wash.
When a bed's to be made I make it.
You may tip me with a penny, and I'll thank you very well
And you see me dressed in tatters, and this tatty old hotel
And you never ask how long I'll take it.
But one of these evenings there will be screams from the harbour
And they'll ask: what can all that screaming be?
And they'll see me smiling as I do the glasses
And they'll say: how she can smile beats me.
    And a ship with eight sails and
    All its fifty guns loaded
    Has tied up at the quay.

They say: get on, dry your glasses, my girl
And they tip me and don't give a damn.
And their penny is accepted, and their bed will be made
(Although nobody is going to sleep there, I'm afraid)
And they still have no idea who I am.
But one of these evenings there will be explosions from the
   harbour,
And they'll ask: what kind of a bang was that?
And they'll see me as I stand beside the window
And they'll say: what has she got to smile at?
    And that ship with eight sails and
    All its fifty guns loaded
    Will lay siege to the town.

Then you gents, you aren't going to find it a joke
For the walls will be knocked down flat
And in no time the town will be rased to the ground.
Just one tatty old hotel will be left standing safe and sound
And they'll ask: did someone special live in that?
Then there'll be a lot of people milling round the hotel
And they'll ask: what made them let that place alone?

And they'll see me as I leave the door next morning
And they'll say: don't tell us she's the one.
>   And that ship with eight sails and
>   All its fifty guns loaded
>   Will run up its flag.

And a hundred men will land in the bright midday sun
Each stepping where the shadows fall.
They'll look inside each doorway and grab anyone they see
And put him in irons and then bring him to me
And they'll ask: which of these should we kill?
In that noonday heat there'll be a hush round the harbour
As they ask which has got to die.
And you'll hear me as I softly answer: the lot!
And as the first head rolls I'll say: hoppla!
>   And that ship with eight sails and
>   All its fifty guns loaded
>   Will vanish with me.

MATTHEW: Very nice. Cute, eh? The way the missus puts it across!

MAC: What do you mean nice? It's not nice, you idiot! It's art, it's not nice. You did that marvellously, Polly. But it's wasted on trash like this, if you'll excuse me, your Reverence. *In an undertone to Polly:* Anyway, I don't like you play-acting; let's not have any more of it.

Laughter at the table. The gang is making fun of the parson.
What you got in your hand, your Reverence?

JAKE: Two knives, Captain.

MAC: What you got on your plate, your Reverence?

KIMBALL: Salmon, I think.

MAC: And with that knife you are eating the salmon, are you not?

JAKE: Did you ever see the like of it, eating fish with a knife? Anybody who does that is just a plain . . .

MAC: Swine. Do you understand me, Jake? Think about it.

JIMMY *rushing in:* Hey, Captain, coppers. The sheriff in person.

WALTER: Brown. Tiger Brown!

MAC: Yes, Tiger Brown, exactly. It's Tiger Brown himself, the Chief Sheriff of London, pillar of the Old Bailey, who will now enter Captain Macheath's humble abode. Think about it. *The bandits creep away.*

JAKE: It'll be the drop for us!
Brown enters.

MAC: Hullo, Jackie.

BROWN: Hullo, Mac! I haven't much time, got to be leaving in a minute. Does it have to be somebody else's stable? Why, this is breaking and entering again!

MAC: But Jackie, it's such a good address. I'm glad you could come to old Mac's wedding. Let me introduce my wife, née Peachum. Polly, this is Tiger Brown, what do you say, old man? *Slaps him on the back.* And these are my friends, Jackie, I imagine you've seen them all before.

BROWN *pained:* I'm here unofficially, Mac.

MAC: So are they. *He calls them. They come in with their hands up.* Hey, Jake.

BROWN: That's Crook-fingered Jake. He's a dirty dog.

MAC: Hey, Jimmy; hey, Bob; hey, Walter!

BROWN: Well, just for today I'll turn a blind eye.

MAC: Hey, Ned; hey, Matthew.

BROWN: Be seated, gentlemen, be seated.

ALL: Thank you, sir.

BROWN: I'm delighted to meet my old friend Mac's charming wife.

POLLY: Don't mention it, sir.

MAC: Sit down, you old bugger, and pitch into the whisky!— Polly and gentlemen! You have today in your midst a man whom the king's inscrutable wisdom has placed high above his fellow men and who has none the less remained my friend throughout the storms and perils, and so on. You know who I mean, and you too know who I mean, Brown. Ah, Jackie, do you remember how we served in India together, soldiers both of us? Ah, Jackie, let's sing the Cannon Song right now. *They sit down on the table.*

Song lighting: golden glow. The organ is lit up. Three lamps are lowered from above on a pole, and the signs say:

THE CANNON SONG

John was all present and Jim was all there
And Georgie was up for promotion.
Not that the army gave a bugger who they were
When confronting some heathen commotion.
> The troops live under
> The cannon's thunder
> From the Cape to Cooch Behar.
> Moving from place to place
> When they come face to face
> With a different breed of fellow
> Whose skin is black or yellow
> They quick as winking chop him into beefsteak tartare.

Johnny found his whisky too warm
And Jim found the weather too balmy
But Georgie took them both by the arm
And said: never let down the army.
> The troops live under
> The cannon's thunder
> From the Cape to Cooch Behar.
> Moving from place to place
> When they come face to face
> With a different breed of fellow
> Whose skin is black or yellow
> They quick as winking chop him into beefsteak tartare.

John is a write-off and Jimmy is dead
And they shot poor old Georgie for looting
But young men's blood goes on being red
And the army goes on recruiting.
> The troops live under
> The cannon's thunder

From the Cape to Cooch Behar.
Moving from place to place
When they come face to face
With a different breed of fellow
Whose skin is black or yellow
They quick as winking chop him into beefsteak tartare.

MAC: Though life with its raging torrent has carried us boy-hood friends far apart, although our professional interests are very different, some people would go so far as to say diametrically opposed, our friendship has come through unimpaired. Think about it. Castor and Pollux, Hector and Andromache, etcetera. Seldom have I, the humble bandit, well, you know what I mean, made even the smallest haul without giving him, my friend, a share, a substantial share, Brown, as a gift and token of my unswerving loyalty, and seldom has he, take that knife out of your mouth, Jake, the all-powerful police chief, staged a raid without sending me, his boyhood friend, a little tip-off. Well, and so on and so forth, it's all a matter of give and take. Think about it. *He takes Brown by the arm.* Well, Jackie, old man, I'm glad you've come, I call that real friendship. *Pause, because Brown has been looking sadly at a carpet.* Genuine Shiraz.

BROWN: From the Oriental Carpet Company.

MAC: Yes, we never go anywhere else. Do you know, Jackie, I had to have you here today, I hope it's not awkward for you in your position?

BROWN: You know, Mac, that I can't refuse you anything. I must be going, I've really got so much on my plate; if the slightest thing should go wrong at the Queen's Coronation . . .

MAC: See here, Jackie, my father-in-law is a revolting old bastard. If he tries to make trouble for me, is there anything on record against me at Scotland Yard?

BROWN: There's nothing whatsoever on record against you at Scotland Yard.

MAC: I knew it.

BROWN: I've taken care of that. Good night.

MAC: Aren't you fellows going to stand up?

BROWN *to Polly:* Best of luck. *Goes out accompanied by Mac.*

JAKE *who along with Matthew and Walter has meanwhile been conferring with Polly:* I must admit I couldn't repress a certain alarm a while ago when I heard Tiger Brown was coming.

MATTHEW: You see, dear lady, we have contacts in the highest places.

WALTER: Yes, Mac always has some iron in the fire that the rest of us don't even suspect. But we have our own little iron in the fire. Gentlemen, it's half-past nine.

MATTHEW: And now comes the *pièce de résistance.*
All go upstage behind the carpet that conceals something. Mac enters.

MAC: I say, what's going on?

MATTHEW: Hey, Captain, another little surprise.
Behind the curtain they sing the Bill Lawgen song softly and with much feeling. But at 'his name was one thing she'd rather like to know' Matthew pulls down the carpet and all go on with the song, bellowing and pounding on the bed that has been disclosed.

MAC: Thank you, friends, thank you.

WALTER: And now we shall quietly take our leave.
The gang go out.

MAC: And now the time has come for softer sentiments. Without them man is a mere beast of burden. Sit down, Polly.
Music.

MAC: Look at the moon over Soho.

POLLY: I see it, dearest. Feel my heart beating, my beloved.

MAC: I feel it, beloved.

POLLY: Where'er you go I shall be with you.

MAC: And where you stay, there too shall I be.

BOTH:
> And though we've no paper to say we're wed
> And no altar covered with flowers

And nobody knows for whom your dress was made
And even the ring is not ours—
The platter off which you've been eating your bread
Give it one brief look; fling it far.
For love will endure or not endure
Regardless of where we are.

3

TO PEACHUM, CONSCIOUS OF THE HARDNESS OF THE WORLD, THE LOSS OF HIS DAUGHTER MEANS UTTER RUIN.

Peachum's Outfitting Emporium for Beggars.

To the right Peachum and Mrs Peachum. In the doorway stands Polly in her coat and hat, holding her travelling bag.

MRS PEACHUM: Married? First you rig her fore and aft in dresses and hats and gloves and parasols, and when she's cost as much as a sailing ship, she throws herself in the garbage like a rotten pickle. Are you really married?
Song lighting: golden glow. The organ is lit up. Three lamps are lowered from above on a pole and the signs say:

IN A LITTLE SONG POLLY GIVES HER PARENTS TO UNDERSTAND THAT SHE HAS MARRIED THE BANDIT MACHEATH:

I once used to think, in my innocent youth
(And I once was as innocent as you)
That someone someday might come my way
And then how should I know what's best to do?
And if he'd got money
And seemed a nice chap
And his workday shirts were white as snow
And if he knew how to treat a girl with due respect
I'd have to tell him: No.

That's where you must keep your head screwed on

And insist on going slow.
Sure, the moon will shine throughout the night
Sure, the boat is on the river, tied up tight.
That's as far as things can go.
Oh, you can't lie back, you must stay cold at heart
Oh, you must not let your feelings show.
Oh, whenever you feel it might start
Ah, then your only answer's: No.

The first one that came was a man of Kent
And all that a man ought to be.
The second one owned three ships down at Wapping
And the third was crazy about me.
And as they'd got money
And all seemed nice chaps
And their workday shirts were white as snow
And as they knew how to treat a girl with due respect
Each time I told them: No.
That's where I still kept my head screwed on
And I chose to take it slow.
Sure, the moon could shine throughout the night
Sure, the boat was on the river, tied up tight
That's as far as things could go.
Oh, you can't lie back, you must stay cold at heart
Oh, you must not let your feelings show.
Oh, whenever you feel it might start
Ah, then your only answer's: No.

But then one day, and that day was blue
Came someone who didn't ask at all
And he went and hung his hat on the nail in my little attic
And what happened I can't quite recall.
And as he'd got no money
And was not a nice chap
And his Sunday shirts, even, were not like snow
And as he'd no idea of treating a girl with due respect
I could not tell him: No.

That's the time my head was not screwed on
And to hell with going slow.
Oh, the moon was shining clear and bright
Oh, the boat kept drifting downstream all that night
That was how it simply had to go.
Yes, you must lie back, you can't stay cold at heart
In the end you have to let your feelings show.
Oh, the moment you know it must start
Ah, then's no time for saying: No.

PEACHUM: So she's associating with criminals. That's lovely. That's delightful.

MRS PEACHUM: If you're immoral enough to get married, did it have to be a horse-thief and a highwayman? That'll cost you dear one of these days! I ought to have seen it coming. Even as a child she had a swollen head like the Queen of England.

PEACHUM: So she's really got married!

MRS PEACHUM: Yes, yesterday, at five in the afternoon.

PEACHUM: To a notorious criminal. Come to think of it, it shows that the fellow is really audacious. If I give away my daughter, the sole prop of my old age, why, my house will cave in and my last dog will run off. I'd think twice about giving away the dirt under my fingernails, it would mean risking starvation. If the three of us can get through the winter on one log of wood, maybe we'll live to see the new year. Maybe.

MRS PEACHUM: What got into you? This is our reward for all we've done, Jonathan. I'm going mad. My head is swimming. I'm going to faint. Oh! *She faints.* A glass of Cordial Médoc.

PEACHUM: You see what you've done to your mother. Quick! Associating with criminals, that's lovely, that's delightful! Interesting how the poor woman takes it to heart. *Polly brings in a bottle of Cordial Médoc.* That's the only consolation your poor mother has left.

POLLY: Go ahead, give her two glasses. *My* mother can take twice as much when she's not quite herself. That will put her back on her feet. *During the whole scene she looks very happy.*

MRS PEACHUM *wakes up:* Oh, there she goes again, pretending
to be so loving and sympathetic!
Five men enter.[5]

BEGGAR: I'm making a complaint, see, this thing is a mess, it's
not a proper stump, it's a botch-up, and I'm not wasting my
money on it.

PEACHUM: What do you expect? It's as good a stump as any
other; it's just that you don't keep it clean.

BEGGAR: Then why don't I take as much money as the others?
Naw, you can't do that to me. *Throws down the stump.* If
I wanted crap like this, I could cut off my real leg.

PEACHUM: What do you fellows want anyway? Is it my fault if
people have hearts of flint? I can't make you five stumps. In
five minutes I can turn any man into such a pitiful wreck it
would make a dog weep to see him. Is it my fault if people
don't weep? Here's another stump for you if one's not enough.
But look after your equipment!

BEGGAR: This one will do.

PEACHUM *tries a false limb on another:* Leather is no good,
Celia; rubber is more repulsive. *To the third:* That swelling is
going down and it's your last. Now we'll have to start all over
again. *Examining the fourth:* Of course natural scabies is
never as good as the artificial kind. *To the fifth:* You're a sight!
You've been eating again. I'll have to make an example of you.

BEGGAR: Mr Peachum, I really haven't eaten anything much.
I'm just abnormally fat, I can't help it.

PEACHUM: Nor can I. You're fired. *Again to the second beggar:*
My dear man, there's an obvious difference between 'tugging
at people's heart strings' and 'getting on people's nerves'. Yes,
artists, that's what I need. Only an artist can tug at anybody's
heart strings nowadays. If you fellows performed properly,
your audience would be forced to applaud. You just haven't
any ideas! Obviously I can't extend your engagement.
The beggars go out.

POLLY: Look. Is he particularly handsome? No. But he makes a
living. He can support me. He is not only a first-class burglar
but a far-sighted and experienced stick-up man as well. I've

been into it, I can tell you the exact amount of his savings to date. A few successful ventures and we shall be able to retire to a little house in the country just like that Mr Shakespeare father admires so much.

PEACHUM: It's quite simple. You're married. What does a girl do when she's married? Use your head. Well, she gets divorced, see. Is that so hard to figure out?

POLLY: I don't know what you're talking about.

MRS PEACHUM: Divorce.

POLLY: But I love him. How can I think of divorce?

MRS PEACHUM: Really, have you no shame?

POLLY: Mother, if you've ever been in love . . .

MRS PEACHUM: In love! Those damn books you've been reading have turned your head. Why, Polly, everybody's doing it.

POLLY: Then I'm an exception.

MRS PEACHUM: Then I'm going to tan your behind, you exception.

POLLY: Oh yes, all mothers do that, but it doesn't help because love goes deeper than a tanned behind.

MRS PEACHUM: Don't strain my patience.

POLLY: I won't let my love be taken away from me.

MRS PEACHUM: One more word out of you and you'll get a clip on the ear.

POLLY: But love is the finest thing in the world.

MRS PEACHUM: Anyway, he's got several women, the blackguard. When he's hanged, like as not half a dozen widows will turn up, each of them like as not with a brat in her arms. Oh, Jonathan!

PEACHUM: Hanged, what made you think of that, that's a good idea. Run along, Polly. *Polly goes out.* Quite right. That'll earn us forty pounds.

MRS PEACHUM: I see. Report him to the sheriff.

PEACHUM: Naturally. And besides, that way we get him hanged free of charge . . . Two birds with one stone. Only we've got to find out where he's holed up.

MRS PEACHUM: I can tell you that, my dear, he's holed up with his tarts.

PEACHUM: But they won't turn him in.

MRS PEACHUM: Just let me attend to that. Money rules the world. I'll go to Turnbridge right away and talk to the girls. Give us a couple of hours, and after that if he meets a single one of them he's done for.

POLLY *has been listening behind the door:* Dear Mama, you can spare yourself the trip. Mac will go to the Old Bailey of his own accord sooner than meet any of those ladies. And even if he did go to the Old Bailey, the sheriff would serve him a cocktail; they'd smoke their cigars and have a little chat about a certain shop in this street where a little more goes on than meets the eye. Because, Papa dear, the sheriff was very cheerful at my wedding.

PEACHUM: What's this sheriff called?

POLLY: He's called Brown. But you probably know him as Tiger Brown. Because everyone who has reason to fear him calls him Tiger Brown. But my husband, you see, calls him Jackie. Because to him he's just dear old Jackie. They're boyhood friends.

PEACHUM: Oh, so they're friends, are they? The sheriff and Public Enemy No. 1, ha, they must be the only friends in this city.

POLLY *poetically:* Every time they drank a cocktail together, they stroked each other's cheeks and said: 'If you'll have the same again, I'll have the same again.' And every time one of them left the room, the other's eyes grew moist and he said: 'Where'er you go I shall be with you.' There's nothing on record against Mac at Scotland Yard.

PEACHUM: I see. Between Tuesday evening and Thursday morning Mr Macheath, a gentleman who has assuredly been married many times, lured my daughter from her home on pretext of marriage. Before the week is out, he will be taken to the gallows on that account, and deservedly so. 'Mr Macheath, you once had white kid gloves, a cane with an ivory handle, and a scar on your neck, and frequented the Cuttlefish Hotel. All that is left is your scar, undoubtedly the least valuable of your distinguishing marks, and today you frequent nothing but prison cells, and within the foreseeable future no place at all . . .'

MRS PEACHUM: Oh, Jonathan, you'll never bring it off. Why, he's Mac the Knife, whom they call the biggest criminal in London. He takes what he pleases.

PEACHUM: Who's Mac the Knife? Get ready, we're going to see the Sheriff of London. And you're going to Turnbridge.

MRS PEACHUM: To see his whores.

PEACHUM: For the villainy of the world is great, and a man needs to run his legs off to keep them from being stolen from under him.

POLLY: I, Papa, shall be delighted to shake hands with Mr Brown again.

All three step forward and sing the first finale. Song lighting. On the signs is written:

FIRST THREE-PENNY FINALE CONCERNING THE
INSECURITY OF THE HUMAN CONDITION

POLLY:

> Am I reaching for the sky?
> All I'm asking from this place is
> To enjoy a man's embraces.
> Is that aiming much too high?

PEACHUM *with a Bible in his hand:*

> Man has a right, in this our brief existence
> To call some fleeting happiness his own
> Partake of worldly pleasures and subsistence
> And have bread on his table rather than a stone.
> Such are the basic rights of man's existence.
> But do we know of anything suggesting
> That when a thing's a right one gets it? No!
> To get one's rights would be most interesting
> But our condition's such it can't be so.

MRS PEACHUM:

> How I want what's best for you
> How I'd teach you airs and graces

Show you things and take you places
As a mother likes to do.

PEACHUM:

Let's practise goodness: who would disagree?
Let's give our wealth away: is that not right?
Once all are good His Kingdom is at hand
Where blissfully we'll bask in His pure light.
Let's practise goodness: who would disagree?
But sadly on this planet while we're waiting
The means are meagre and the morals low.
To get one's record straight would be elating
But our condition's such it can't be so.

POLLY AND MRS PEACHUM:

So that is all there is to it.
The world is poor, and man's a shit.

PEACHUM:

Of course that's all there is to it.
The world is poor, and man's a shit.
Who wouldn't like an earthly paradise?
Yet our condition's such it can't arise.
Out of the question in our case.
Let's say your brother's close to you
But if there's not enough for two
He'll kick you smartly in the face.
You think that loyalty's no disgrace?
But say your wife is close to you
And finds she's barely making do
She'll kick you smartly in the face.
And gratitude: that's no disgrace
But say your son is close to you
And finds your pension's not come through
He'll kick you smartly in the face.
And so will all the human race.

POLLY AND MRS PEACHUM:

That's what you're all ignoring
That's what's so bloody boring.

The world is poor, and man's a shit
And that is all there is to it.

PEACHUM:

Of course that's all there is to it
The world is poor, and man's a shit.
We should aim high instead of low
But our condition's such this can't be so.

ALL THREE:

Which means He has us in a trap:
The whole damn thing's a load of crap.

PEACHUM:

The world is poor, and man's a shit
And that is all there is to it.

ALL THREE:

That's what you're all ignoring
That's what's so bloody boring.
That's why He's got us in a trap
And why it's all a load of crap.

ACT TWO

4

The stable.

POLLY *enters:* Mac! Mac, don't be frightened.

MAC *lying on the bed:* Well, what's up? Polly, you look a wreck.

POLLY: I've been to see Brown, my father went too, they decided to pull you in; my father made some terrible threats and Brown stood up for you, but then he weakened, and now he thinks too that you'd better stir yourself and make yourself scarce for a while, Mac. You must pack right away.

MAC: Pack? Nonsense. Come here, Polly. You and I have got better things to do than pack.

POLLY: No, we mustn't now. I'm so frightened. All they talked about was hanging.

MAC: I don't like it when you're moody, Polly. There's nothing on record against me at Scotland Yard.

POLLY: Perhaps there wasn't yesterday, but suddenly today there's an awful lot. You—I've brought the charges with me, I don't even know if I can get them straight, the list goes on so. You've killed two shopkeepers, more than thirty burglaries, twenty-three hold-ups, and God knows how many acts of arson, attempted murder, forgery and perjury, all within eight-

een months. You're a dreadful man. And in Winchester you se-
duced two sisters under the age of consent.

MAC: They told me they were over twenty. What did Brown say?
*He stands up slowly and goes whistling to the right along the
footlights.*

POLLY: He caught up with me in the corridor and said there
was nothing he could do for you now. Oh, Mac! *She throws
herself on his neck.*

MAC: All right, if I've got to go away, you'll have to run the
business.

POLLY: Don't talk about business now, Mac, I can't bear it. Kiss
your poor Polly again and swear that you'll never never be . . .
*Mac interrupts her brusquely and leads her to the table
where he pushes her down in a chair.*

MAC: Here are the ledgers. Listen carefully. This is a list of the
personnel. *Reads.* Hm, first of all, Crook-finger Jake, a year
and a half in the business. Let's see what he's brought in.
One, two, three, four, five gold watches, not much, but clean
work. Don't sit on my lap, I'm not in the mood right now.
Here's Dreary Walter, an unreliable sod. Sells stuff on the
side. Give him three weeks, grace, then get rid of him. Just
turn him in to Brown.

POLLY *sobbing:* Just turn him in to Brown.

MAC: Jimmy II, cheeky bastard; good worker but cheeky.
Swipes bed sheets right out from under ladies of the best society. Give him a rise.

POLLY: I'll give him a rise.

MAC: Robert the Saw: small potatoes, not a glimmer of genius.
Won't end on the gallows, but he won't leave any estate either.

POLLY: Won't leave any estate either.

MAC: In all other respects you will carry on exactly the same
as before. Get up at seven, wash, have your weekly bath and
so on.

POLLY: You're perfectly right, I'll have to grit my teeth and
look after the business. What's yours is mine now, isn't it,
Mackie? What about your chambers, Mac? Should I let them
go? I don't like having to pay the rent.

MAC: No, I still need them.

POLLY: What for, it's just a waste of our money!

MAC: Oh, so you think I won't be coming back at all, do you?

POLLY: What do you mean? You can rent other rooms. Mac . . .
Mac, I can't go on. I keep looking at your lips and then I
don't hear what you say. Will you be faithful to me, Mac?[6]

MAC: Of course I'll be faithful, I'll do as I'm done by. Do you think
I don't love you? It's only that I see farther ahead than you.

POLLY: I'm so grateful to you, Mac. Worrying about me when
they're after you like bloodhounds . . .
*Hearing the word 'bloodhounds' he goes stiff, stands up,
goes to the right, throws off his coat and washes his hands.*

MAC *hastily:* You will go on sending the profits to Jack Poole's
banking house in Manchester. Between ourselves it's only a
matter of weeks before I go over to banking altogether. It's
safer and it's more profitable. In two weeks at the most the
money will have to be taken out of this business, then off you
go to Brown and give the list to the police. Within four weeks
all that human scum will be safely in the cells at the Old Bailey.

POLLY: Why, Mac! How can you look them in the eye when
you've written them off and they're as good as hanged? How
can you shake hands with them?

MAC: With who? Robert the Saw, Matt of the Mint, Crook-
fingered Jake? Those gaol-birds?
Enter the gang.

MAC: Gentlemen, it's a pleasure to see you.

POLLY: Good evening, gentlemen.

MATTHEW: I've got hold of the Coronation programme, Captain. It looks to me like we're going to be very busy in the
next few days. The Archbishop of Canterbury is arriving in
half an hour.

MAC: When?

MATTHEW: Five thirty. We'd better be shoving off, Captain.

MAC: Yes, you'd better be shoving off.

ROBERT: What do you mean: you?

MAC: For my part, I'm afraid I'm obliged to take a little trip.

ROBERT: Good God, are they out to nab you?

MATTHEW: It would be just now, with the Coronation coming up!
A Coronation without you is like porridge without a spoon.

MAC: Shut your trap! In view of that, I am temporarily handing
over the management of the business to my wife.

He pushes her forward and goes to the rear where he observes her.

POLLY: Well, boys, I think the Captain can go away with an
easy mind. We'll swing this job, you bet. What do you say,
boys?

MATTHEW: It's no business of mine. But at a time like this I'm
not so sure that a woman . . . I'm not saying anything against
you, Ma'am.

MAC *from upstage:* What do you say to that, Polly?

POLLY: You shit, that's a fine way to start in. *Screaming.* Of
course you're not saying anything against me! If you were,
these gentlemen would have ripped your pants off long ago
and tanned your arse for you. Wouldn't you, gentlemen?
Brief pause, then all clap like mad.

JAKE: Yes, there's something in that, you can take her word for it.

WALTER: Hurrah, the missus knows how to lay it on! Hurrah
for Polly!

ALL: Hurrah for Polly!

MAC: The rotten part of it is that I won't be here for the Coronation. There's a gilt-edged deal for you. In the day time nobody's home and at night the toffs are all drunk. That reminds
me, you drink too much, Matthew. Last week you suggested
it was you set the Greenwich Children's Hospital on fire. If
such a thing occurs again, you're out. Who set the Children's
Hospital on fire?

MATTHEW: I did.

MAC *to the others:* Who set it on fire?

THE OTHERS: You, Mr Macheath.

MAC: So who did it?

MATTHEW *sulkily:* You, Mr Macheath. At this rate our sort
will never rise in the world.

MAC *with a gesture of stringing up:* You'll rise all right if you
think you can compete with me. Who ever heard of one of

those professors at Oxford College letting some assistant put his name to his mistakes? He puts his own.

ROBERT: Ma'am, while your husband is away, you're the boss. We settle up every Thursday, ma'am.

POLLY: Every Thursday, boys.

The gang goes out.

MAC: And now farewell, my heart. Look after your complexion, and don't forget to make up every day, exactly as if I were here. That's very important, Polly.

POLLY: And you, Mac, promise me you won't look at another woman and that you'll leave town right away. Believe me, it's not jealousy that makes your little Polly say that; no, it's very important, Mac.

MAC: Oh, Polly, why should I go round drinking up the empties? I love only you. As soon as the twilight is deep enough I'll take my black stallion from somebody's stable and before you can see the moon from your window, I'll be the other side of Highgate Heath.

POLLY: Oh, Mac, don't tear the heart out of my body. Stay with me and let us be happy.

MAC: But I must tear my own heart out of my body, for I must go away and no one knows when I shall return.

POLLY: It's been such a short time, Mac.

MAC: Does it have to be the end?

POLLY: Oh, last night I had a dream. I was looking out the window and I heard laughter in the street, and when I looked out I saw our moon and the moon was all thin like a worn-down penny. Don't forget me, Mac, in strange cities.

MAC: Of course I won't forget you, Polly. Kiss me, Polly.

POLLY: Goodbye, Mac.

MAC: Goodbye, Polly. *On his way out:*

> For love will endure or not endure
> Regardless of where we are.

POLLY *alone:* He never will come back. *She sings:*

> Nice while it lasted, and now it is over
> Tear out your heart, and goodbye to your lover!
> What's the use of grieving, when the mother that bore you

(Mary, pity women!) knew it all before you?
The bells start ringing.

POLLY:

Into this London the Queen now makes her way.
Where shall we be on Coronation Day?

Interlude

Mrs Peachum and Low-Dive Jenny step out before the curtain.

MRS PEACHUM: So if you see Mac the Knife in the next few days, run to the nearest constable and turn him in; it'll earn you ten shillings.

JENNY: Shall we see him, though, if the constables are after him? If the hunt is on, he won't go spending his time with us.

MRS PEACHUM: Take it from me, Jenny, even with all London at his heels, Macheath is not the man to give up his habits. *She sings:*

THE BALLAD OF SEXUAL OBSESSION

There goes a man who's won his spurs in battle
The butcher, he. And all the others, cattle.
The cocky sod! No decent place lets him in.
Who does him down, that's done the lot? The women.
Want it or not, he can't ignore that call.
Sexual obsession has him in its thrall.
    He doesn't read the Bible. He sniggers at the law
    Sets out to be an utter egoist
    And knows a woman's skirts are what he must resist
    So when a woman calls he locks his door.
    So far, so good, but what's the future brewing?
    As soon as night falls he'll be up and doing.

Thus many a man watched men die in confusion:
A mighty genius, stuck on prostitution!

The watchers claimed their urges were exhausted
But when they died who paid the funeral? Whores did.
Want it or not, they can't ignore that call.
Sexual obsession has them in its thrall.
 Some fall back on the Bible. Some stick to the law
 Some turn to Christ and some turn anarchist.
 At lunch you pick the best wine on the list
 Then meditate till half-past four.
 At tea: what high ideals you are pursuing!
 Then soon as night falls you'll be up and doing.

5

BEFORE THE CORONATION BELLS HAD DIED AWAY, MAC THE KNIFE WAS SITTING WITH THE WHORES OF TURNBRIDGE! THE WHORES BETRAY HIM. IT IS THURSDAY EVENING.

Whorehouse in Turnbridge.

An afternoon like any other; the whores, mostly in their shifts, are ironing clothes, playing draughts, or washing: a bourgeois idyll.[7] *Crook-fingered Jake is reading the newspaper. No one pays any attention to him. He is rather in the way.*

JAKE: He won't come today.
WHORE: No?
JAKE: I don't think he'll ever come again.
WHORE: That would be a pity.
JAKE: Think so? If I know him, he's out of town by now. This time he's really cleared out.
 Enter Macheath, hangs his hat on a nail, sits down on the sofa behind the table.
MAC: My coffee!
VIXEN *repeats admiringly:* 'My coffee!'
JAKE *horrified:* Why aren't you in Highgate?

MAC: It's my Thursday. Do you think I can let such trifles inter-
fere with my habits? *Throws the warrant on the floor.* Any-
how, it's raining.

JENNY *reads the warrant:* In the name of the King, Captain
Macheath is charged with three . . .

JAKE *takes it away from her:* Am I in it too?

MAC: Naturally, the whole team.

JENNY *to the other whore:* Look, that's the warrant. *Pause.*
Mac, let's see your hand. *He gives her his hand.*

DOLLY: That's right, Jenny, read his palm, you do it so well.
Holds up an oil lamp.

MAC: Coming into money?

JENNY: No, not coming into money.

BETTY: What's that look for, Jenny? It gives me the shivers.

MAC: A long journey?

JENNY: No, no long journey.

VIXEN: What *do* you see?

MAC: Only the good things, not the bad, please.

JENNY: Oh well, I see a narrow dark place and not much light.
And then I see a big T, that means a woman's treachery. And
then I see . . .

MAC: Stop. I'd like some details about that narrow dark place
and the treachery. What's this treacherous woman's name?

JENNY: All I see is it begins with a J.

MAC: Then you've got it wrong. It begins with a P.

JENNY: Mac, when the Coronation bells start ringing at Westminster, you'll be in for a sticky time.

MAC: Go on! *Jake laughs uproariously.* What's the matter? *He
runs over to Jake, and reads.* They've got it wrong, there
were only three of them.

JAKE *laughs:* Exactly.

MAC: Nice underwear you've got there.

WHORE: From the cradle to the grave, underwear first, last and
all the time.

OLD WHORE: I never wear silk. Makes gentlemen think you've
got something wrong with you.
Jenny slips stealthily out the door.

SECOND WHORE *to Jenny:* Where are you going, Jenny?

JENNY: You'll see. *Goes out.*

DOLLY: But homespun underwear can put them off too.

OLD WHORE: I've had very good results with homespun underwear.

VIXEN: It makes the gentlemen feel they're at home.

MAC *to Betty:* Have you still got the black lace trimming?

BETTY: Still the black lace trimming.

MAC: What kind of lingerie do you have?

SECOND WHORE: Oh, I don't like to tell you. I can't take anybody to my room because my aunt is so crazy about men, and in doorways, you know, I just don't wear any.
Jake laughs.

MAC: Finished?

JAKE: No, I just got to the rapes.

MAC *back to the sofa:* But where's Jenny? Ladies, long before my star rose over this city . . .

VIXEN: 'Long before my star rose over this city . . .'

MAC: . . . I lived in the most impecunious circumstances with one of you dear ladies. And though today I am Mac the Knife, my good fortune will never lead me to forget the companions of my dark days, especially Jenny, whom I loved the best of all. Now listen, please.
While Mac sings, Jenny stands to the right outside the window and beckons to Constable Smith. Then Mrs Peachum joins her. The three stand under the street lamp and watch the house.

BALLAD OF IMMORAL EARNINGS

There was a time, now very far away
When we set up together, I and she.
I'd got the brain, and she supplied the breast.
I saw her right, and she looked after me—
A way of life then, if not quite the best.
And when a client came I'd slide out of our bed
And treat him nice, and go and have a drink instead

And when he paid up I'd address him: Sir
Come any night you feel you fancy her.
That time's long past, but what would I not give
To see that whorehouse where we used to live?
Jenny appears in the door, with Smith behind her.

JENNY:

That was the time, now very far away
He was so sweet and bashed me where it hurt.
And when the cash ran out the feathers really flew
He'd up and say: I'm going to pawn your skirt.
A skirt is nicer, but no skirt will do.
Just like his cheek, he had me fairly stewing
I'd ask him straight to say what he thought he was doing
Then he'd lash out and knock me headlong down the stairs.
I had the bruises off and on for years.

BOTH:

That time's long past, but what would I not give
To see that whorehouse where we used to live?

BOTH *together and alternating:*

That was the time, now very far away[8]

MAC:

Not that the bloody times seem to have looked up.

JENNY:

When afternoons were all I had for you

MAC:

I told you she was generally booked up.
(The night's more normal, but daytime will do.)

JENNY:

Once I was pregnant, so the doctor said.

MAC:

So we reversed positions on the bed.

JENNY:

He thought his weight would make it premature.

MAC:

But in the end we flushed it down the sewer.
That could not last, but what would I not give
To see that whorehouse where we used to live?

Dance. Mac picks up his sword stick, she hands him his hat, he is still dancing when Smith lays a hand on his shoulder.

SMITH: Coming quietly?

MAC: Is there only one way out of this dump?

Smith tries to put the handcuffs on Macheath; Mac gives him a push in the chest and he reels back. Mac jumps out of the window. Outside stands Mrs Peachum with constables.

MAC *with poise, very politely:* Good afternoon, ma'am.

MRS PEACHUM: My dear Mr Macheath. My husband says the greatest heroes in history have tripped over this humble threshold.

MAC: May I ask how your husband is doing?

MRS PEACHUM: Better, thank you. I'm so sorry, you'll have to be bidding the charming ladies goodbye now. Come, constable, escort the gentleman to his new home. *He is led away. Mrs Peachum through the window:* Ladies, if you wish to visit him, you'll invariably find him in. From now on the gentleman's address will be the Old Bailey. I knew he'd be round to see his whores. I'll settle the bill. Goodbye, ladies. *Goes out.*

JENNY: Wake up, Jake, something has happened.

JAKE *who has been too immersed in his reading to notice anything:* Where's Mac?

JENNY: The rozzers were here.

JAKE: Good God! And me just reading, reading, reading . . . Well, I never! *Goes out.*

6

BETRAYED BY THE WHORES, MACHEATH IS FREED
FROM PRISON BY THE LOVE OF YET ANOTHER WOMAN.

The cells in the Old Bailey.
A cage.

Enter Brown.

BROWN: If only my men don't catch him! Let's hope to God
he's riding out beyond Highgate Heath, thinking of his
Jackie. But he's so frivolous, like all great men. If they bring
him in now and he looks at me with his faithful friendly eyes,
I won't be able to bear it. Thank God, anyway, the moon is
shining; if he is riding across the heath, at least he won't stray
from the path. *Sounds backstage.* What's that? Oh, my God,
they're bringing him in.

MAC *tied with heavy ropes, accompanied by six constables, enters
with head erect.* Well, flatfeet, thank God we're home again.
He notices Brown who has fled to the far corner of the cell.

BROWN *after a long pause, under the withering glance of his
former friend:* Oh, Mac, it wasn't me . . . I did everything . . . don't look at me like that, Mac . . . I can't stand
it . . . Your silence is killing me. *Shouts at one of the constables:* Stop tugging at that rope, you swine . . . Say something,
Mac. Say something to your poor Jackie . . . A kind word in
his tragic . . . *Rests his head against the wall and weeps.* He
doesn't deem me worthy even of a word. *Goes out.*

MAC: That miserable Brown. The living picture of a bad conscience. And he calls himself a chief of police. It was a good
idea not shouting at him. I was going to at first. But just in time
it occurred to me that a deep withering stare would send much
colder shivers down his spine. It worked. I looked at him and
he wept bitterly. That's a trick I got from the Bible.
Enter Smith with handcuffs.

MAC: Well, Mr Warder, I suppose these are the heaviest you've got? With your kind permission I should like to apply for a more comfortable pair. *He takes out his cheque book.*

SMITH: Of course, Captain, we've got them here at every price. It all depends how much you want to spend. From one guinea to ten.

MAC: How much would none at all be?

SMITH: Fifty.

MAC *writes a cheque:* But the worst of it is that now this business with Lucy is bound to come out. If Brown hears that I've been carrying on with his daughter behind his friendly back, he'll turn into a tiger.

SMITH: You've made your bed, now lie on it.

MAC: I bet the little tart is waiting outside right now. I can see happy days between now and the execution.

Is this a life for one of my proud station?
I take it, I must frankly own, amiss.
From childhood up I heard with consternation:

One must live well to know what living is!
Song lighting: golden glow. The organ is lit up. Three lamps are lowered on a pole, and the signs say:

BALLADE OF GOOD LIVING[9]

I've heard them praising single-minded spirits
Whose empty stomachs show they live for knowledge
In rat-infested shacks awash with ullage.
I'm all for culture, but there are some limits.
The simple life is fine for those it suits.
I don't find, for my part, that it attracts.
There's not a bird from here to Halifax
Would peck at such unappetising fruits.
What use is freedom? None, to judge from this.
One must live well to know what living is.

The dashing sort who cut precarious capers
And go and risk their necks just for the pleasure
Then swagger home and write it up at leisure
And flog the story to the Sunday papers—
If you could see how cold they get at night
Sullen, with chilly wife, climbing to bed
And how they dream they're going to get ahead
And see the future stretching out of sight—
Now tell me, who would choose to live like this?
One must live well to know what living is.

There's plenty that they have. I know I lack it
And ought to join their splendid isolation
But when I gave it more consideration
I told myself: my friend, that's not your racket.
Suffering ennobles, but it can depress.
The paths of glory lead but to the grave.
You once were poor and lonely, wise and brave.
You ought to try to bite off rather less.
The search for happiness boils down to this:
One must live well to know what living is.

Enter Lucy.

LUCY: You dirty dog, you—how can you look me in the face after all there's been between us?

MAC: Have you no bowels, no tenderness, my dear Lucy, seeing a husband in such circumstances?

LUCY: A husband! You monster! So you think I haven't heard about your goings-on with Miss Peachum! I could scratch your eyes out!

MAC: Seriously, Lucy, you're not fool enough to be jealous of Polly?

LUCY: You're married to her, aren't you, you beast?

MAC: Married! It's true, I go to the house, I chat with the girl. I kiss her, and now the silly jade goes about telling everyone that I'm married to her. I am ready, my dear Lucy, to give you satisfaction—if you think there is any in marriage.

What can a man of honour say more? He can say nothing
more.

LUCY: Oh, Mac, I only want to become an honest woman.

MAC: If you think marriage with me will . . . all right. What
can a man of honour say more? He can say nothing more.
Enter Polly.

POLLY: Where is my dear husband? Oh, Mac, there you are.
Why do you turn away from me? It's your Polly. It's your wife.

LUCY: Oh, you miserable villain!

POLLY: Oh, Mackie in prison! Why didn't you ride across
Highgate Heath? You told me you weren't going to see
those women any more. I knew what they'd do to you; but I
said nothing, because I believed you. Mac, I'll stay with you
till death us do part.—Not one kind word, Mac? Not one
kind look? Oh, Mac, think what your Polly must be suffering to see you like this.

LUCY: Oh, the slut.

POLLY: What does this mean, Mac? Who on earth is that? You
might at least tell her who I am. Please tell her I'm your wife.
Aren't I your wife? Look at me. Tell me, aren't I your wife?

LUCY: You low-down sneak! Have you got two wives, you
monster?

POLLY: Say something, Mac. Aren't I your wife? Haven't I
done everything for you? I was innocent when I married, you
know that. Why, you even put me in charge of the gang, and
I've done it all the way we arranged, and Jake wants me to
tell you that he . . .

MAC: If you two would kindly shut your traps for one minute
I'll explain everything.

LUCY: No, I won't shut my trap, I can't bear it. It's more than
flesh and blood can stand.

POLLY: Yes, my dear, naturally the wife has . . .

LUCY: The wife!!

POLLY: . . . the wife is entitled to some preference. Or at least
the appearance of it, my dear. All this fuss and bother will
drive the poor man mad.

LUCY: Fuss and bother, that's a good one. What have you gone

and picked up now? This messy little tart! So this is your
great conquest! So this is your Rose of old Soho!
*Song lighting: golden glow. The organ is lit up. Three lamps
are lowered on a pole and the signs say:*

JEALOUSY DUET

LUCY:

Come on out, you Rose of Old Soho!

Let us see your legs, my little sweetheart!

I hear you have a lovely ankle

And I'd love to see such a complete tart.

They tell me that Mac says your behind is so provoking.

POLLY:

Did he now, did he now?

LUCY:

If what I see is true he must be joking.

POLLY:

Is he now, is he now?

LUCY:

Ho, it makes me split my sides!

POLLY:

Oh, that's how you split your side?

LUCY:

Fancy you as Mackie's bride!

POLLY:

Mackie fancies Mackie's bride.

LUCY:

Ha ha ha! Catch him sporting

With something that the cat brought in.

POLLY:

Just you watch your tongue, my dear.

LUCY:

Must I watch my tongue, my dear?

BOTH:

Mackie and I, see how we bill and coo, man

He's got no eye for any other woman.

The whole thing's an invention
You mustn't pay attention
To such a bitch's slanders.
Poppycock!

POLLY:

Oh, they call me Rose of Old Soho
And Macheath appears to find me pretty.

LUCY:

Does he now?

POLLY:

They say I have a lovely ankle
And the best proportions in the city.

LUCY:

Little whippersnapper!

POLLY:

Who's a little whippersnapper?
Mac tells me that he finds my behind is most provoking.

LUCY:

Doesn't he? Doesn't he?

POLLY:

I do not suppose that he is joking.

LUCY:

Isn't he, isn't he?

POLLY:

Ho, it makes me split my sides!

LUCY:

Oh, that's how you split your side?

POLLY:

Being Mackie's only bride!

LUCY:

Are you Mackie's only bride?

POLLY *to the audience*:

Can you really picture him sporting
With something that the cat brought in?

LUCY:

Just you watch your tongue, my dear.

POLLY:

Must I watch my tongue, my dear?

BOTH:

Mackie and I, see how we bill and coo, man

He's got no eye for any other woman.

The whole thing's an invention

You cannot pay attention

To such a bitch's slanders.

Poppycock!

MAC: All right, Lucy. Calm down. You see it's just a trick of Polly's. She wants to come between us. I'm going to be hanged and she wants to parade as my widow. Really, Polly, this isn't the moment.

POLLY: Have you the heart to disclaim me?

MAC: And have you the heart to go on about my being married? Oh, Polly, why do you have to add to my misery? *Shakes his head reproachfully:* Polly! Polly!

LUCY: It's true, Miss Peachum. You're putting yourself in a bad light. Quite apart from the fact that it's uncivilised of you to worry a gentleman in his situation!

POLLY: The most elementary rules of decency, my dear young lady, ought to teach you, it seems to me, to treat a man with a little more reserve when his wife is present.

MAC: Seriously, Polly, that's carrying a joke too far.

LUCY: And if, my dear lady, you start raising a row here in this prison, I shall be obliged to send for the screw to show you the door. I'm sorry, my dear Miss Peachum.

POLLY: Mrs, if you please! Mrs Macheath. Just let me tell you this, young lady. The airs you give yourself are most unbecoming. My duty obliges me to stay with my husband.

LUCY: What's that? What's that? Oh, she won't leave! She stands there and we throw her out and she won't leave! Must I speak more plainly?

POLLY: You—you just hold your filthy tongue, you slut, or I'll knock your block off, my dear young lady.

LUCY: You've been thrown out, you interloper! I suppose that's not clear enough. You don't understand nice manners.

POLLY: You and your nice manners! Oh, I'm forgetting my dignity! I shouldn't stoop to . . . no, I shouldn't.
She starts to bawl.

LUCY: Just look at my belly, you slut! Did I get that from out of nowhere? Haven't you eyes in your head?

POLLY: Oh! So you're in the family way! And you think that gives you rights? A fine lady like you, you shouldn't have let him in!

MAC: Polly!

POLLY *in tears:* This is really too much. Mac, you shouldn't have done that. Now I don't know what to do.
Enter Mrs Peachum.

MRS PEACHUM: I knew it. She's with her man. You little trollop, come here immediately. When they hang your man, you can hang yourself too. A fine way to treat your respectable mother, making her come and get you out of jail. And he's got two of them, what's more—the Nero!

POLLY: Leave me here, mama; you don't know . . .

MRS PEACHUM: You're coming home this minute.

LUCY: There you are, it takes your mama to tell you how to behave.

MRS PEACHUM: Get going.

POLLY: Just a second. I only have to . . . I only have to tell him something . . . Really . . . it's very important.

MRS PEACHUM *giving her a box on the ear:* Well, this is important too. Get going!

POLLY: Oh, Mac! *She is dragged away.*

MAC: Lucy, you were magnificent. Of course I felt sorry for her. That's why I couldn't treat the slut as she deserved. Just for a moment you thought there was some truth in what she said. Didn't you?

LUCY: Yes, my dear, so I did.

MAC: If there were any truth in it, her mother wouldn't have put me in this situation. Did you hear how she laid into me? A mother might treat a seducer like that, not a son-in-law.

LUCY: It makes me happy to hear you say that from the bottom of your heart. I love you so much I'd almost rather see you on the gallows than in the arms of another. Isn't that strange?

MAC: Lucy, I should like to owe you my life.

LUCY: It's wonderful the way you say that. Say it again.

MAC: Lucy, I should like to owe you my life.

LUCY: Shall I run away with you, dearest?

MAC: Well, but you see, if we run away together, it won't be easy for us to hide. As soon as they stop looking, I'll send for you post haste, you know that.

LUCY: What can I do to help you?

MAC: Bring me my hat and cane.

Lucy comes back with his hat and cane and throws them into his cage.

Lucy, the fruit of our love which you bear beneath your heart will hold us forever united.

Lucy goes out.

SMITH *enters, goes into the cell, and says to Mac:* Let's have that cane.

After a brief chase, in which Smith pursues Mac with a chair and a crow bar, Mac jumps over the bars. Constables run after him.

Enter Brown.

BROWN *off:* Hey, Mac!—Mac, answer me, please. It's Jackie. Mac, please be a good boy, answer me, I can't stand it any longer. *Comes in.* Mackie! What's this? He's gone, thank God. *He sits down on the bed.*

Enter Peachum.

PEACHUM *to Smith:* My name is Peachum. I've come to collect the forty pounds reward for the capture of the bandit Macheath. *Appears in front of the cage.* Excuse me! Is that Mr Macheath? *Brown is silent.* Oh. I suppose the other gentleman has gone for a stroll? I come here to visit a criminal

and who do I find sitting here but Mr Brown! Tiger Brown is
sitting here and his friend Macheath is not sitting here.

BROWN *groaning:* Oh, Mr Peachum, it wasn't my fault.

PEACHUM: Of course not. How could it be? You'd never have
dreamt . . . considering the situation it'll land you in . . . it's
out of the question, Brown.

BROWN: Mr Peachum, I'm beside myself.

PEACHUM: I believe you. Terrible, you must feel.

BROWN: Yes, it's this feeling of helplessness that ties one's
hands so. Those fellows do just as they please. It's dreadful,
dreadful.

PEACHUM: Wouldn't you care to lie down awhile? Just close
your eyes and pretend nothing has happened. Imagine you're
on a lovely green meadow with little white clouds overhead.
The main thing is to forget all about those ghastly things, those
that are past, and most of all, those that are still to come.

BROWN *alarmed:* What do you mean by that?

PEACHUM: I'm amazed at your fortitude. In your position I
should simply collapse, crawl into bed and drink hot tea. And
above all, I'd find someone to lay a soothing hand on my
forehead.

BROWN: Damn it all, it's not my fault if the fellow escapes.
There's not much the police can do about it.

PEACHUM: I see. There's not much the police can do about it.
You don't believe we'll see Mr Macheath back here again?
Brown shrugs his shoulders. In that case your fate will be
hideously unjust. People are sure to say—they always do—
that the police shouldn't have let him escape. No, I can't see
that glittering Coronation procession just yet.

BROWN: What do you mean?

PEACHUM: Let me remind you of a historical incident which,
though it caused a great stir at the time, in the year 1400 BC,
is unknown to the public of today. On the death of the Egyptian king Rameses II, the police captain of Nineveh, or was it
Cairo, committed some minor offence against the lower classes
of the population. Even at that time the consequences were terrible. As the history books tell us, the coronation procession

of Semiramis, the new Queen, 'developed into a series of catastrophes thanks to the unduly active participation of the
lower orders'. Historians still shudder at the cruel way Semiramis treated her police captain. I only remember dimly, but
there was some talk of snakes she fed on his bosom.

BROWN: Really?

PEACHUM: The Lord be with you, Brown. *Goes out.*

BROWN: Now only the mailed fist can help. Sergeants! Report
to me at the double!

*Curtain. Macheath and Low-Dive Jenny step before the cur-
tain and sing to song lighting:*

SECOND THREEPENNY FINALE
WHAT KEEPS MANKIND ALIVE?

You gentlemen who think you have a mission
To purge us of the seven deadly sins
Should first sort out the basic food position
Then start your preaching: that's where it begins.
You lot, who preach restraint and watch your waist as well
Should learn for all time how the world is run:
However much you twist, whatever lies you tell
Food is the first thing. Morals follow on.
So first make sure that those who now are starving
Get proper helpings when we do the carving.
  What keeps mankind alive? The fact that millions
  Are daily tortured, stifled, punished, silenced, oppressed.
  Mankind can keep alive thanks to its brilliance
  In keeping its humanity repressed.
  For once you must try not to shirk the facts:
  Mankind is kept alive by bestial acts.

You say that girls may strip with your permission.
You draw the lines dividing art from sin.
So first sort out the basic food position
Then start your preaching: that's where we begin.
You lot, who bank on your desires and our disgust

Should learn for all time how the world is run:
Whatever lies you tell, however much you twist
Food is the first thing. Morals follow on.
So first make sure that those who now are starving
Get proper helpings when we do the carving.

> What keeps mankind alive? The fact that millions
> Are daily tortured, stifled, punished, silenced, oppressed.
> Mankind can keep alive thanks to its brilliance
> In keeping its humanity repressed.
> For once you must try not to shirk the facts:
> Mankind is kept alive by bestial acts.

ACT THREE

7

THAT NIGHT PEACHUM PREPARES HIS CAMPAIGN.
HE PLANS TO DISRUPT THE CORONATION PROCESSION
BY A DEMONSTRATION OF HUMAN MISERY.

Peachum's Outfitting Emporium for Beggars.

The beggars paint little signs with inscriptions such as 'I gave my eye for my king', etc.

PEACHUM: Gentlemen, at this moment, in our eleven branches from Drury Lane to Turnbridge, one thousand four hundred and thirty-two gentlemen are working on signs like these with a view to attending the Coronation of our Queen.

MRS PEACHUM: Get a move on! If you won't work, you can't beg. Call yourself a blind man and can't even make a proper K? That's supposed to be child's writing, anyone would think it was an old man's.
A drum rolls.

BEGGAR: That's the Coronation guard presenting arms. Little do they suspect that today, the biggest day in their military careers, they'll have us to deal with.

FILCH *enters and reports:* Mrs Peachum, there's a dozen sleepy-looking hens traipsing in. They claim there's some money due them.
Enter the whores.

JENNY: Madam . . .

MRS PEACHUM: Hm, you do look as if you'd fallen off your perches. I suppose you've come to collect the money for that Macheath of yours? Well, you'll get nothing, you understand, nothing.

JENNY: How are we to understand that, Ma'am?

MRS PEACHUM: Bursting in here in the middle of the night! Coming to a respectable house at three in the morning! With the work you do, I should think you'd want some sleep. You look like sicked-up milk.

JENNY: Then you won't give us the stipulated fee for turning in Macheath, ma'am?

MRS PEACHUM: Exactly. No thirty pieces of silver for you.

JENNY: Why not, ma'am?

MRS PEACHUM: Because your fine Mr Macheath has scattered himself to the four winds. And now, ladies, get out of my parlour.

JENNY: Well, I call that the limit. Just don't you try that on us. That's all I've got to say to you. Not on us.

MRS PEACHUM: Filch, the ladies wish to be shown the door.

Filch goes towards the ladies, Jenny pushes him away.

JENNY: I would be grateful if you would be so good as to hold your filthy tongue. If you don't, I'm likely to . . .

Enter Peachum.

PEACHUM: What's going on, you haven't given them any money, I hope? Well, ladies how about it? Is Mr Macheath in jail, or isn't he?

JENNY: Don't talk to me about Mr Macheath. You're not fit to black his boots. Last night I had to let a customer go because it made me cry into my pillow thinking how I had sold that gentleman to you. Yes, ladies, and what do you think happened this morning? Less than an hour ago, just after I had cried myself to sleep, I heard somebody whistle, and out on the street stood the very gentleman I'd been crying about, asking me to throw down the key. He wanted to lie in my arms and make me forget the wrong I had done him. Ladies, he's the last sportsman left in London. And if our friend Suky

Tawdry isn't here with us now, it's because he went on from me to her to console her too.

PEACHUM *muttering to himself:* Suky Tawdry ...

JENNY: So now you know that you're not fit to black that gentleman's boots. You miserable sneak.

PEACHUM: Filch, run to the nearest police station, tell them Mr Macheath is at Miss Suky Tawdry's place. *Filch goes out.* But ladies, what are we arguing for? The money will be paid out, that goes without saying. Celia dear, you'd do better to make the ladies some coffee instead of slanging them.

MRS PEACHUM *on her way out:* Suky Tawdry! *She sings the third stanza of the Ballad of Sexual Obsession:*

There stands a man. The gallows loom above him.
They've got the quicklime mixed in which to shove him.
They've put his neck just under where the noose is
And what's he thinking of, the idiot? Floozies.
They've all but hanged him, yet he can't ignore that call.
Sexual obsession has him in its thrall.
    She's sold him down the river heart and soul
    He's seen the dirty money in her hand
    And bit by bit begins to understand:
    The pit that covers him is woman's hole.
    Then he may rant and roar and curse his ruin—
    But soon as night falls he'll be up and doing.

PEACHUM: Get a move on, you'd all be rotting in the sewers of Turnbridge if in my sleepless nights I hadn't worked out how to squeeze a penny out of your poverty. I discovered that though the rich of this earth find no difficulty in creating misery, they can't bear to see it. Because they are weaklings and fools just like you. They may have enough to eat till the end of their days, they may be able to wax their floors with butter so that even the crumbs from their tables grow fat. But they can't look on unmoved while a man is collapsing from hunger, though of course that only applies so long as he collapses outside their own front door.

Enter Mrs Peachum with a tray full of coffee cups.

MRS PEACHUM: You can come by the shop tomorrow and pick up your money, but only once the Coronation's over.

JENNY: Mrs Peachum, you leave me speechless.

PEACHUM: Fall in. We assemble in one hour outside Buckingham Palace. Quick march.

The beggars fall in.

FILCH *dashes in:* Cops! I didn't even get to the police station. The police are here already.

PEACHUM: Hide, gentlemen! *To Mrs Peachum:* Call the band together. Shake a log. And if you hear me say 'harmless', do you understand, *harmless . . .*

MRS PEACHUM: Harmless? I don't understand a thing.

PEACHUM: Naturally you don't understand. Well, if I say *harmless . . . Knocking at the door.* Thank God, that's the answer, *harmless*, then you play some kind of music. Get a move on! *Mrs Peachum goes out with the beggars. The beggars, except for the girl with the sign 'A Victim of Military Tyranny', hide with their things upstage right behind the clothes rack. Enter Brown and constables.*

BROWN: Here we are. And now, Mr Beggar's Friend, drastic action will be taken. Put the derbies on him, Smith. Ah, here are some of those delightful signs. *To the girl:* 'A Victim of Military Tyranny'—is that you?

PEACHUM: Good morning, Brown, good morning. Sleep well?

BROWN: Huh?

PEACHUM: Morning, Brown.

BROWN: Is he saying that to me? Does he know one of you? I don't believe I have the pleasure of your acquaintance.

PEACHUM: Really? Morning, Brown.

BROWN: Knock his hat off. *Smith does so.*

PEACHUM: Look here, Brown, since you're passing by, *passing*, I say, Brown, I may as well ask you to put a certain Macheath under lock and key, it's high time.

BROWN: The man's mad. Don't laugh, Smith. Tell me, Smith, how is it possible that such a notorious criminal should be running around loose in London?

PEACHUM: Because he's your pal, Brown.

BROWN: Who?

PEACHUM: Mac the Knife. Not me. I'm no criminal. I'm a poor man, Brown. You can't abuse me, Brown, you've got the worst hour in your life ahead of you. Care for some coffee? *To the whores:* Girls, give the chief of police a sip, that's no way to behave. Let's all be friends. We are all law-abiding people. The law was made for one thing alone, for the exploitation of those who don't understand it, or are prevented by naked misery from obeying it. And anyone who wants a crumb of this exploitation for himself must obey the law strictly.

BROWN: I see, then you believe our judges are corruptible?

PEACHUM: Not at all, sir, not at all. Our judges are absolutely incorruptible: it's more than money can do to make them give a fair verdict.

A second drum roll.

The troops are marching off to line the route. The poorest of the poor will move off in half an hour.

BROWN: That's right, Mr Peachum. In half an hour the poorest of the poor will be marched off to winter quarters in the Old Bailey. *To the constables:* All right, boys, round them all up, all the patriots you find here. *To the beggars:* Have you fellows ever heard of Tiger Brown? Tonight, Peachum, I've hit on the solution, and I believe I may say, saved a friend from mortal peril. I'll simply smoke out your whole nest. And lock up the lot of you for—hm, for what? For begging on the street. You seem to have intimated your intention of embarrassing me and the Queen with these beggars. I shall simply arrest the beggars. Think about it.

PEACHUM: Excellent, but . . . what beggars?

BROWN: These cripples here. Smith, we're taking these patriots along with us.

PEACHUM: I can save you from a hasty step; you can thank the
Lord, Brown, that you came to me. You see, Brown, you can
arrest these few, they're harmless, *harmless . . . Music starts
up, playing a few measures of the 'Song of the Insufficiency
of Human Endeavour'.*
BROWN: What's that?
PEACHUM: Music. They're playing as well as they can. The
Song of Insufficiency. You don't know it? Think about it.
*Song lighting: golden glow. The organ is lit up. Three lamps
are lowered from above on a pole and the signs say:*

SONG OF THE INSUFFICIENCY OF HUMAN ENDEAVOUR

Mankind lives by its head
Its head won't see it through
Inspect your own. What lives off that?
At most a louse or two.
    For this bleak existence
    Man is never sharp enough.
    Hence his weak resistance
    To its tricks and bluff.

Aye, make yourself a plan
They need you at the top!
Then make yourself a second plan
Then let the whole thing drop.
    For this bleak existence
    Man is never bad enough
    Though his sheer persistence
    Can be lovely stuff.

Aye, race for happiness
But don't you race too fast.
When all start chasing happiness
Happiness comes in last.

For this bleak existence
Man is never undemanding enough.
All his loud insistence
Is a load of guff.

PEACHUM: Your plan, Brown, was brilliant but hardly realistic. All you can arrest in this place is a few young fellows celebrating their Queen's Coronation by arranging a little fancy dress party. When the real paupers come along—there aren't any here—there will be thousands of them. That's the point: you've forgotten what an immense number of poor people there are. When you see them standing outside the Abbey, it won't be a festive sight. You see, they don't look good. Do you know what grogblossom is, Brown? Yes, but how about a hundred and twenty noses all flushed with grogblossom? Our young Queen's path should be strewn with blossom, not with grogblossom. And all those cripples at the church door. That's something one wishes to avoid, Brown. You'll probably say the police can handle us poor folk. You don't believe that yourself. How will it look if six hundred poor cripples have to be clubbed down at the Coronation? It will look bad. It will look disgusting. Nauseating. I feel faint at the thought of it, Brown. A small chair, if you please.

BROWN *to Smith:* That's a threat. See here, you, that's blackmail. We can't touch the man, in the interests of public order we simply can't touch him. I've never seen the like of it.

PEACHUM: You're seeing it now. Let me tell you something. You can behave as you please to the Queen of England. But you can't tread on the toes of the poorest man in England, or you'll be brought down, Mr Brown.

BROWN: So you're asking me to arrest Mac the Knife? Arrest him? That's easy to say. You have to find a man before you can arrest him.

PEACHUM: If you say that, I can't contradict you. So I'll find your man for you; we'll see if there's any morality left. Jimmy, where is Mr Macheath at this moment?

JENNY: 21 Oxford Street, at Suky Tawdry's.

BROWN: Smith, go at once to Suky Tawdry's place at 21 Oxford Street, arrest Macheath and take him to the Old Bailey. In the meantime, I must put on my gala uniform. On this day of all days I must wear my gala uniform.

PEACHUM: Brown, if he's not on the gallows by six o'clock . . .

BROWN: Oh, Mac, it was not to be. *Goes out with constables.*

PEACHUM *calling after him:* Think about it, eh, Brown?

Third drum roll.

Third drum roll. Change of objective. You will head for the dungeons of the Old Bailey.

The beggars go out.

Peachum sings the fourth stanza of the 'Song of Human Insufficiency':

Man could be good instead
So slug him on the head
If you can slug him good and hard
He may stay good and dead.
    For this bleak existence
    Man's not good enough just yet.
    You'll need no assistance.
    Slug him on the head.

Curtain. Jenny steps before the curtain with a hurdy-gurdy and sings the

SOLOMON SONG

You saw sagacious Solomon
You know what came of him.
To him complexities seemed plain.
He cursed the hour that gave birth to him
And saw that everything was vain.
How great and wise was Solomon!
But now that time is getting late

The world can see what followed on.
It's wisdom that had brought him to this state—
How fortunate the man with none!

You saw the lovely Cleopatra
You know what she became.
Two emperors slaved to serve her lust.
She whored herself to death and fame
Then rotted down and turned to dust.
How beautiful was Babylon!
But now that time is getting late
The world can see what followed on.
It's beauty that had brought her to this state—
How fortunate the girl with none!

You saw the gallant Caesar next
You know what he became.
They deified him in his life
Then had him murdered just the same.
And as they raised the fatal knife
How loud he cried 'You too, my son!'
But now that time is getting late
The world can see what followed on.
It's courage that had brought him to this state—
How fortunate the man with none!

You know the ever-curious Brecht
Whose songs you liked to hum.
He asked, too often for your peace
Where rich men get their riches from.
So then you drove him overseas.
How curious was my mother's son!
But now that time is getting late
The world can see what followed on.
Inquisitiveness brought him to this state—
How fortunate the man with none!

And now look at this man Macheath
The sands are running out.
If only he'd known where to stop
And stuck to crimes he knew all about
He surely would have reached the top.
But one fine day his heart was won.
So now that time is getting late
The world can see what followed on.
His sexual urges brought him to this state—
How fortunate the man with none!

8

PROPERTY IN DISPUTE.[10]

A young girl's room in the Old Bailey.

Lucy.

SMITH *enters:* Miss, Mrs Polly Macheath wishes to speak with you.
LUCY: Mrs Macheath? Show her in.
Enter Polly.
POLLY: Good morning, madam. Madam, good morning.
LUCY: What is it, please?
POLLY: Do you recognise me?
LUCY: Of course I know you.
POLLY: I've come to beg your pardon for the way I behaved yesterday.
LUCY: Very interesting.
POLLY: I have no excuse to offer for my behaviour, madam, but my misfortunes.
LUCY: I see.
POLLY: Madam, you must forgive me. I was stung by Mr Macheath's behaviour. He really should not have put us in such a situation, and you can tell him so when you see him.

LUCY: I . . . I . . . shan't be seeing him.

POLLY: Of course you will see him.

LUCY: I shall not see him.

POLLY: Forgive me.

LUCY: But he's very fond of you.

POLLY: Oh no, you're the only one he loves. I'm sure of that.

LUCY: Very kind of you.

POLLY: But, madam, a man is always afraid of a woman who loves him too much. And then he's bound to neglect and avoid her. I could see at a glance that he is more devoted to you than I could ever have guessed.

LUCY: Do you mean that sincerely?

POLLY: Of course, certainly, very sincerely, madam. Do believe me.

LUCY: Dear Miss Polly, both of us have loved him too much.

POLLY: Perhaps. *Pause.* And now, madam, I want to tell you how it all came about. Ten days ago I met Mr Macheath for the first time at the Cuttlefish Hotel. My mother was there too. Five days later, about the day before yesterday, we were married. Yesterday I found out that he was wanted by the police for a variety of crimes. And today I don't know what's going to happen. So you see, madam, twelve days ago I couldn't have imagined ever losing my heart to a man.
Pause.

LUCY: I understand, Miss Peachum.

POLLY: Mrs Macheath.

LUCY: Mrs Macheath.

POLLY: To tell the truth, I've been thinking about this man a good deal in the last few hours. It's not so simple. Because you see, Miss, I really can't help envying you for the way he behaved to you the other day. When I left him, only because my mother made me, he didn't show the slightest sign of regret. Maybe he has no heart and nothing but a stone in his breast. What do you think, Lucy?

LUCY: Well, my dear Miss, I really don't know if Mr Macheath is entirely to blame. You should have stuck to your own class of people, dear Miss.

POLLY: Mrs Macheath.

LUCY: Mrs Macheath.

POLLY: That's quite true—or at least, as my father always advised me, I should have kept everything on a strict business footing.

LUCY: Definitely.

POLLY *weeping:* But he's my only possession in all the world.

LUCY: My dear, such a misfortune can befall the most intelligent woman. But after all, you are his wife on paper. That should be a comfort to you. Poor child, I can't bear to see you so depressed. Won't you have a little something?

POLLY: What?

LUCY: Something to eat.

POLLY: Oh yes, please, a little something to eat. *Lucy goes out. Polly aside:* The hypocritical strumpet.

LUCY *comes back with coffee and cake:* Here. This ought to do it.

POLLY: You really have gone to too much trouble, madam. *Pause. She eats.* What a lovely picture of him you've got. When did he bring it?

LUCY: Bring it?

POLLY *innocently:* I mean when did he bring it up here to you?

LUCY: He didn't bring it.

POLLY: Did he give it to you right here in this room?

LUCY: He never was in this room.

POLLY: I see. But there wouldn't have been any harm in that. The paths of fate are so dreadfully crisscrossed.

LUCY: Must you keep talking such nonsense? You only came here to spy.

POLLY: Then you know where he is?

LUCY: Me? Don't you know?

POLLY: Tell me this minute where he is.

LUCY: I have no idea.

POLLY: So you don't know where he is. Word of honour?

LUCY: No, I don't know. Hm, and you don't either?

POLLY: No. This is terrible. *Polly laughs and Lucy weeps.* Now he has two commitments. And he's gone.

LUCY: I can't stand it any more. Oh, Polly, it's so dreadful.

POLLY *gaily:* I'm so happy to have found such a good friend at the end of this tragedy. That's something. Would you care for a little more to eat? Some more cake?

LUCY: Just a bit! Oh, Polly, don't be so good to me. Really, I don't deserve it. Oh, Polly, men aren't worth it.

POLLY: Of course men aren't worth it, but what else can we do?

LUCY: No! Now I'm going to make a clean breast of it. Will you be very cross with me, Polly?

POLLY: About what?

LUCY: It's not real!

POLLY: What?

LUCY: This here! *She indicates her belly.* And all for that crook!

POLLY *laughs:* Oh, that's magnificent! Is it a cushion? Oh, you really are a hypocritical strumpet! Look—you want Mackie? I'll make you a present of him. If you find him you can keep him. *Voices and steps are heard in the corridor.* What's that?

LUCY *at the window:* Mackie! They've caught him once more.

POLLY *collapses:* This is the end.

Enter Mrs Peachum.

MRS PEACHUM: Ha, Polly, so this is where I find you. You must change your things, your husband is being hanged. I've brought your widow's weeds. *Polly changes into the widow's dress.* You'll be a lovely widow. But you'll have to cheer up a little.

9

FRIDAY MORNING. 5 AM. MAC THE KNIFE, WHO HAS BEEN WITH THE WHORES AGAIN, HAS AGAIN BEEN BETRAYED BY WHORES. HE IS ABOUT TO BE HANGED.

Death cell.

The bells of Westminster ring. Constables bring Macheath shackled into the cell.

SMITH: Bring him in here. Those are the bells of Westminster. Stand up straight, I'm not asking you why you look so worn out. I'd say you were ashamed. *To the constables:* When the bells of Westminster ring for the third time, that will be at six, he's got to have been hanged. Make everything ready.

A CONSTABLE: For the last quarter of an hour all the streets around Newgate have been so jammed with people of all classes you can't get through.

SMITH: Strange! Then they already know?

CONSTABLE: If this goes on, the whole of London will know in another quarter of an hour. All the people who would otherwise have gone to the Coronation will come here. And the Queen will be riding through empty streets.

SMITH: All the more reason for us to move fast. If we're through by six, that will give people time to get back to the Coronation by seven. So now, get going.

MAC: Hey, Smith, what time is it?

SMITH: Haven't you got eyes? Five oh-four.

MAC: Five oh-four.

Just as Smith is locking the cell door from outside, Brown enters.

BROWN, *his back to the cell, to Smith:* Is he in there?

SMITH: You want to see him?

BROWN: No, no, no, for God's sake. I'll leave it all to you. *Goes out.*

MAC *suddenly bursts into a soft unbroken flow of speech:* All right, Smith, I won't say a word, not a word about bribery, never fear. I know all about it. If you let yourself be bribed, you'd have to leave the country for a start. You certainly would. You'd need enough to live on for the rest of your life. A thousand pounds, eh? Don't say anything! In twenty minutes I'll tell you whether you can have your thousand pounds by noon. I'm not saying a word about feelings. Go outside and think it over carefully. Life is short and money is scarce. And I don't even know yet if I can raise any. But if anyone wants to see me, let them in.

SMITH *slowly:* That's a lot of nonsense, Mr Macheath. *Goes out.*

MAC *sings softly and very fast the 'Call from the Grave':*

Hark to the voice that's calling you to weep.

Macheath lies here, not under open sky

Not under treetops, no, but good and deep.

Fate struck him down in outraged majesty.

God grant his dying words may reach a friend.

The thickest walls encompass him about.

Is none of you concerned to know his fate?

Once he is gone the bottles can come out

But do stand by him while it's not too late.

D'you want his punishment to have no end?[11]

Matthew and Jake appear in the corridor. They are on their way to see Macheath. Smith stops them.

SMITH: Well, son. You look like a soused herring.

MATTHEW: Now the captain's gone it's my job to put our girls in pod, so they can throw themselves on the mercy of the court. It's a job for a horse. I've got to see the Captain.

Both continue towards Mac.

MAC: Five twenty-five. You took your time.

JAKE: Yes, but, you see, we had to . . . [12]

MAC: You see, you see. I'm being hanged, man! But I've no time to waste arguing with you. Five twenty-eight. All right: How much can you people draw from your savings account right away?

MATTHEW: From our . . . at five o'clock in the morning?

JAKE: Has it really come to this?

MAC: Can you manage four hundred pounds?

JAKE: But what about us? That's all there is.

MAC: Who's being hanged, you or me?

MATTHEW *excitedly:* Who was lying around with Suky Tawdry instead of clearing out? Who was lying around with Suky Tawdry, us or you?

MAC: Shut your trap. I'll soon be lying somewhere other than with that slut. Five-thirty.

JAKE: Matt, if that's how it is, we'll just have to do it.

SMITH: Mr Brown wishes to know what you'd like for your . . . repast.

MAC: Don't bother me. *To Matthew:* Well, will you or won't you? *To Smith:* Asparagus.

MATTHEW: Don't you shout at me. I won't have it.

MAC: I'm not shouting at you. It's only that . . . well, Matthew, are you going to let me be hanged?

MATTHEW: Of course I'm not going to let you be hanged. Who said I was? But that's the lot. Four hundred pounds is all there is. No reason why I shouldn't say that, is there?

MAC: Five thirty-eight.

JAKE: We'll have to run, Matthew, or it'll be no good.

MATTHEW: If we can only get through. There's such a crowd. Human scum! *Both go out.*

MAC: If you're not here by five to six, you'll never see me again. *Shouts:* You'll never see me again . . .

SMITH: They've gone. Well, how about it? *Makes a gesture of counting money.*

MAC: Four hundred. *Smith goes out shrugging his shoulders. Mac, calling after him:* I've got to speak to Brown.

SMITH *comes back with constables:* Got the soap?

CONSTABLE: Yes, but not the right kind.

SMITH: You can set the thing up in ten minutes.

CONSTABLE: But the trap doesn't work.

SMITH: It's got to work. The bells have gone a second time.

CONSTABLE: What a shambles!

MAC *sings:*
    Come here and see the shitty state he's in.
    This really is what people mean by bust.
    You who set up the dirty cash you win
    As just about the only god you'll trust
    Don't stand and watch him slipping round the bend!
    Go to the Queen and say that her subjects need her
    Go in a group and tell her of his trouble
    Like pigs all following behind their leader.
    Say that his teeth are wearing down to rubble.
    D'you want his punishment to have no end?

SMITH: I can't possibly let you in. You're only number sixteen. Wait your turn.

POLLY: What do you mean, number sixteen? Don't be a bureaucrat. I'm his wife. I've got to see him.

SMITH: Not more than five minutes, then.

POLLY: Five minutes! That's perfectly ridiculous. Five minutes! How's a lady to say all she's got to say? It's not so simple. This is goodbye forever. There's an exceptional amount of things for man and wife to talk about at such a moment . . . where is he?

SMITH: What, can't you see him?

POLLY: Oh yes, of course. Thank you.

MAC: Polly!

POLLY: Yes, Mackie, here I am.

MAC: Oh yes, of course!

POLLY: How are you? Are you quite worn out? It's hard.

MAC: But what are you going to do now? What will become of you?

POLLY: Don't worry, the business is doing very well. That's the least part of it. Are you very nervous, Mackie? . . . By the way, what was your father? There's so much you still haven't told me. I just don't understand. Your health has always been excellent.

MAC: Polly, can't you help me to get out?

POLLY: Oh yes, of course.

MAC: With money, of course. I've arranged with the warder . . .

POLLY *slowly:* The money has gone off to Manchester.

MAC: And you have got none on you?

POLLY: No, I have got nothing on me. But you know, Mackie, I could talk to somebody, for instance . . . I might even ask the Queen in person. *She breaks down.* Oh, Mackie!

SMITH *pulling Polly away:* Well, have you raised those thousand pounds?

POLLY: All the best, Mackie, look after yourself, and don't forget me! *Goes out.*

Smith and a constable bring in a table with a dish of asparagus on it.

SMITH: Is the asparagus tender?

CONSTABLE: Yes. *Goes out.*

BROWN *appears and goes up to Smith:* Smith, what does he want me for? It's good you didn't take the table in earlier.

We'll take it right in with us, to show him how we feel about him. *They enter the cell with the table. Smith goes out. Pause.* Hello, Mac. Here's your asparagus. Won't you have some?

MAC: Don't you bother, Mr Brown. There are others to show me the last honours.[13]

BROWN: Oh, Mackie!

MAC: Would you have the goodness to produce your accounts? You don't mind if I eat in the meantime, after all it is my last meal. *He eats.*

BROWN: I hope you enjoy it. Oh, Mac, you're turning the knife in the wound.

MAC: The accounts, sir, if you please, the accounts. No sentimentality.

BROWN *with a sigh takes a small notebook from his pocket:* I've got them right here, Mac. The accounts for the past six months.

MAC *bitingly:* Oh, so all you came for was to get your money before it's too late.

BROWN: You know that isn't so . . .

MAC: Don't worry, sir, nobody's going to cheat you. What do I owe you? But I want a detailed bill, if you don't mind. Life has made me distrustful . . . in your position you should be able to understand that.

BROWN: Mac, when you talk that way I just can't think.

A loud pounding is heard rear.

SMITH *off:* All right, that'll hold.

MAC: The accounts, Brown.

BROWN: Very well, if you insist. Well, first of all the rewards for murderers arrested thanks to you or your men. The Treasury paid you a total of . . .

MAC: Three instances at forty pounds a piece, that makes a hundred and twenty pounds. One quarter for you comes to thirty pounds, so that's what we owe you.

BROWN: Yes . . . yes . . . but really, Mac, I don't think we ought to spend our last . . .

MAC: Kindly stop snivelling. Thirty pounds. And for the job in Dover eight pounds.

BROWN: Why only eight pounds, there was . . .

MAC: Do you believe me or don't you believe me? Your share in the transactions of the last six months comes to thirty-eight pounds.

BROWN *wailing:* For a whole lifetime . . . I could read . . .

BOTH: Your every thought in your eyes.

MAC: Three years in India—John was all present and Jim was all there—five years in London, and this is the thanks I get. *Indicating how he will look when hanged.*

> Here hangs Macheath who never wronged a flea
> A faithless friend has brought him to this pass.
> And as he dangles from the gallowstree
> His neck finds out how heavy is his arse.

BROWN: If that's the way you feel about it, Mac . . . The man who impugns my honour, impugns me. *Runs furiously out of the cage.*

MAC: Your honour . . .

BROWN: Yes, my honour. Time to begin, Smith! Let them in! *To Mac:* Excuse me, would you?

SMITH *quickly to Macheath:* I can still get you out of here, in another minute I won't be able to. Have you got the money?

MAC: Yes, as soon as the boys get back.

SMITH: There's no sign of them. The deal is off.

People are admitted. Peachum, Mrs Peachum, Polly, Lucy, the whores, the parson, Matthew and Jake.

JENNY: They weren't anxious to let us in. But I said to them: If you don't get those pisspots you call heads out of my way, you'll hear from Low-Dive Jenny.

PEACHUM: I am his father-in-law. I beg your pardon, which of the present company is Mr Macheath?

MAC *introduces himself:* I'm Macheath.

PEACHUM *walks past the cage, and like all who follow him stations himself to the right of it:* Fate, Mr Macheath, has decreed that though I don't know you, you should be my son-in-law. The occasion of this first meeting between us is a very sad one. Mr Macheath, you once had white kid gloves, a cane with an ivory handle, and a scar on your neck, and you frequented the Cuttlefish Hotel. All that is left is your scar, no doubt the least valuable of your distinguishing marks. Today you frequent nothing but prison cells, and within the foreseeable future no place at all . . .

Polly passes the cage in tears and stations herself to the right.

MAC: What a pretty dress you're wearing.

Matthew and Jake pass the cage and station themselves on the right.

MATTHEW: We couldn't get through because of the terrible crush. We ran so hard I was afraid Jake was going to have a stroke. If you don't believe us . . .

MAC: What do my men say? Have they got good places?

MATTHEW: You see, Captain, we thought you'd understand. You see, a Coronation doesn't happen every day. They've got to make some money while there's a chance. They send you their best wishes.

JAKE: Their very best wishes.

MRS PEACHUM *steps up to the cage, stations herself on the right:* Mr Macheath, who would have expected this a week ago when we were dancing at a little hop at the Cuttlefish Hotel.

MAC: A little hop.

MRS PEACHUM: But the ways of destiny are cruel here below.

BROWN *at the rear to the parson:* And to think that I stood shoulder to shoulder with this man in Azerbaidjan under a hail of bullets.

JENNY *approaches the cage:* We Drury Lane girls are frantic. Nobody's gone to the Coronation. Everybody wants to see you. *Stations herself on the right.*

MAC: To see me.

SMITH: All right. Let's go. Six o'clock. *Lets him out of the cage.*

MAC: We mustn't keep anybody waiting. Ladies and gentlemen. You see before you a declining representative of a declining social group. We lower middle-class artisans who toil with our humble jemmies on small shopkeepers' cash registers are being swallowed up by big corporations backed by the banks. What's a jemmy compared with a share certificate? What's breaking into a bank compared with founding a bank? What's murdering a man compared with employing a man? Fellow citizens, I hereby take my leave of you. I thank you for coming. Some of you were very close to me. That Jenny should have turned me in amazes me greatly. It is proof positive that the world never changes. A concatenation of several unfortunate circumstances has brought about my fall. So be it—I fall.

Song lighting: golden glow. The organ is lit up. Three lamps are lowered on a pole, and the signs say:

BALLAD IN WHICH MACHEATH BEGS
ALL MEN FOR FORGIVENESS

You fellow men who live on after us
Pray do not think you have to judge us harshly
And when you see us hoisted up and trussed
Don't laugh like fools behind your big moustaches
Or curse at us. It's true that we came crashing
But do not judge our downfall like the courts.
Not all of us can discipline our thoughts—
Dear fellows, your extravagance needs slashing.
Dear fellows, we've shown how a crash begins.
Pray then to God that He forgive my sins.

The rain washes away and purifies.
Let it wash down the flesh we catered for
And we who saw so much, and wanted more—
The crows will come and peck away our eyes.
Perhaps ambition used too sharp a goad
It drove us to these heights from which we swing
Hacked at by greedy starlings on the wing
Like horses' droppings on a country road.
O brothers, learn from us how it begins
And pray to God that He forgive our sins.

The girls who flaunt their breasts as bait there
To catch some sucker who will love them

The youths who slyly stand and wait there
To grab their sinful earnings off them
The crooks, the tarts, the tarts' protectors
The models and the mannequins
The psychopaths, the unfrocked rectors
I pray that they forgive my sins.

Not so those filthy police employees
Who day by day would bait my anger
Devise new troubles to annoy me
And chuck me crusts to stop my hunger.
I'd call on God to come and choke them
And yet my need for respite wins:
I realise that it might provoke them
So pray that they forgive my sins.

Someone must take a huge iron crowbar
And stave their ugly faces in
All I ask is to know it's over
Praying that they forgive my sins.

SMITH: If you don't mind, Mr Macheath.
MRS PEACHUM: Polly and Lucy, stand by your husband in his
last hour.
MAC: Ladies, whatever there may have been between us . . .
SMITH *leads him away:* Get a move on!
Procession to the Gallows.
*All go out through doors left. These doors are on projection
screens. Then all re-enter from the other side of the stage
with dark lanterns. When Macheath is standing at the top of
the gallows steps Peachum speaks.*

Dear audience, we now are coming to
The point where we must hang him by the neck
Because it is the Christian thing to do
Proving that men must pay for what they take.

But as we want to keep our fingers clean
And you're the people we can't risk offending
We thought we'd better do without this scene
And substitute instead a different ending.

Since this is opera, not life, you'll see
Justice give way before humanity.
So now, to stop our story in its course
Enter the royal official on his horse.

THIRD THREEPENNY FINALE APPEARANCE OF
THE DEUS EX MACHINA

CHORUS:

Hark, who's here?
A royal official on horseback's here!
Enter Brown on horseback as deus ex machina.

BROWN: I bring a special order from our beloved Queen to have Captain Macheath set at liberty forthwith—*All cheer.*—as it's the coronation, and raised to the hereditary peerage. *Cheers.* The castle of Marmarel, likewise a pension of ten thousand pounds, to be his in usufruct until his death. To any bridal couples present Her Majesty bids me to convey her gracious good wishes.

MAC:

Reprieved! Reprieved! I was sure of it.
When you're most despairing
The clouds may be clearing

POLLY: Reprieved, my dearest Macheath is reprieved. I am so happy.

MRS PEACHUM: So it all turned out nicely in the end. How nice and easy everything would be if you could always reckon with saviours on horseback.

PEACHUM: Now please remain all standing in your places, and join in the hymn of the poorest of the poor, whose most arduous lot you have put on stage here today. In real life the fates they meet can only be grim. Saviours on horseback are seldom met with in practice. And the man who's kicked about must kick back. Which all means that injustice should be spared from persecution.

All come forward, singing to the organ:

> Injustice should be spared from persecution:
> Soon it will freeze to death, for it is cold.
> Think of the blizzards and the black confusion
> Which in this vale of tears we must behold.

The bells of Westminster are heard ringing for the third time.

NOTES AND VARIANTS

Texts by Brecht

ADDITIONAL SONGS FROM 'THE BRUISE'

Second Part

After Mr Peachum and his friend Macheath have left, Mr Brown sings these stanzas to the 'Mac the Knife' time:

Oh, they're such delightful people
As long as no one interferes
While they battle for the loot which
Doesn't happen to be theirs.

When the poor man's lamb gets butchered
If two butchers are involved
Then the fight between those butchers
By the police must be resolved.

Third Part

As they drive up in four or five automobiles the gang sing:

SONG TO INAUGURATE THE NATIONAL DEPOSIT BANK

Don't you think a bank's foundation
Gives good cause for jubilation?
Those who hadn't a rich mother
Must raise cash somehow or other.
To that end stocks serve much better
Than your swordstick or biretta
But what lands you in the cart
Is getting capital to start.

If you've got none, why reveal it?
All you need to do is steal it.
Don't all banks get started thanks to
Doing as the other banks do?
How did all that money come there?—
They'll have taken it from somewhere.

*And Mr Macheath walks with a light step in the direction of the West In-
dia Dock . . . humming a few new verses to an instantly obsolete ballad:*

How's mankind to get some money?
In his office, cold like snow
Sits the banker Mac the Knife, but he
Isn't asked, and ought to know.

In Hyde Park behold a ruined
Man reclining in the sun
(While down Piccadilly, hat and cane, just think about it)
Strolls the banker Mac the Knife, and
God alone knows what he's done.

Fourth Part

CLOSING VERSES OF THE BALLAD

So we reach our happy ending.
Rich and poor can now embrace.
Once the cash is not a problem
Happy endings can take place.

Smith says Jones should be indicted
Since his business isn't straight.
Over luncheon, reunited
See them clear the poor man's plate.

Some in light and some in darkness
That's the kind of world we mean.
Those you see are in the light part.
Those in darkness don't get seen.

[From 'Die Beule' in Brecht; *Versuche*, re-edition 1959, pp. 229 ff., and
GW *Texts für Film* pp. 329 ff. This was Brecht's proposed treatment for

Pabst's *Threepenny Opera* film, for which see the introduction (p. xxxvi). In the Second Part the police also sing the 'Whitewash Song' subsequently used in the Berliner Ensemble production of *Arturo Ui*. Excepting the re-use of the Mac the Knife ballad, there were no settings to these songs by Weill. Three of them also occur in *The Threepenny Novel*.]

APPENDIX

NEW CLOSING VERSES TO THE BALLAD OF MAC THE KNIFE

And the fish keep disappearing
And the Law's perturbed to hear
When at last the shark's arrested
That the shark has no idea.

And there's nothing he remembers
And there's nothing to be done
For a shark is not a shark if
Nobody can prove he's one.

THE NEW CANNON SONG

1

Fritz joined the Party and Karl the S.A.
And Albert was up for selection
Then they were told they must put all that away
And they drove off in every direction.
    Müller from Prussia
    Requires White Russia
    Paris will meet Schmidt's needs.
    Moving from place to place
    Avoiding face to face
    Contact with foreign forces
    Equipped with tanks or horses
    Why, Meier from Berlin is bound to
    End up in Leeds.

2

Müller found the desert too hot
And Schmidt didn't like the Atlantic.
Will they ever see home? That's the problem they've got

And it's making them perfectly frantic.
    To get from Russia
    Back home to Prussia
    From Tunis to Landshut:
    Moving from place to place
    Once they come face to face
    With nasty foreign forces
    Equipped with tanks or horses
    Their leader gives no lead because he's
    Gone off for good.

3

Müller was killed, and the Germans didn't win
And the rats ran around in the rubble.
All the same, in the ruins of Berlin
They're expecting a *third* lot of trouble.
    Cologne is dying
    Hamburg is crying
    And Dresden's past all hope.
    But once the U.S.A.
    Sees Russia's in its way
    With a bit of luck that ought to
    Set off a new bout of slaughter
    And Meier, back in uniform, might
    Get the whole globe!

BALLAD OF THE GOOD LIVING OF HITLER'S MINIONS

I

That drug-crazed Reich Marshal, who killed and jested
You saw half Europe scoured by him for plunder
Then watched him sweat at Nuremberg—and no wonder—
Outbulging those by whom he'd been arrested.
And when they asked him what he did it for
The man replied: for Germany alone.
So that can make a man weigh twenty stone?
Don't pull my leg; I've heard that one before.
No, what made him a Nazi was just this:
One must live well to know what living is.

2

Then Schacht, the Doctor who took out your money—
The sheer length of his neck still has me baffled—

As banker once he fed on milk and honey
As bankrupter he's sure to dodge the scaffold.
He knows he won't be tortured, anyway
But ask Schacht, now he's finally been floored
Just why he joined the others in their fraud
He'll say ambition made him go astray.
But we know what pushed him to the abyss:
One must live well to know what living is.

3

And Keitel, who left the Ukraine all smoking
And licked the Führer's boots clean with his spittle
Because he'd built the Wehrmacht up a little—
Ask that tank expert why, he'll think you're joking.
Sipping, he'll say: I followed Duty's call!
So Duty made his casualties so great?
No question of acquiring an estate:
That kind of thing we don't discuss at all.
We get one. 'How?' 's a question we dismiss.
One must live well to know what living is.

4

They all have great ideas in untold numbers
And lay claim to the loftiest of wishes
And none of them mentions the list of dishes
But each of them has demons plague his slumbers.
Each saw himself no doubt as Lohengrin
Or Parsifal; so how was he to fail?
Behind Moscow they sought the Holy Grail
And just Valhalla crumbled, not Berlin.
Their private problems all boiled down to this:
One must live well to know what living is.

NEW VERSION OF THE BALLAD IN WHICH
MACHEATH BEGS FORGIVENESS

You fellow men who want to live, like us
Pray do not think you have to judge us harshly
And when you see us hoisted up and trussed
Don't laugh like fools behind your big moustaches.
Oh, you who've never crashed as we came crashing
Don't castigate our downfall like the courts:

Not all of us can discipline our thoughts—
Dear fellows, your extravagance needs slashing
Dear fellows, we've shown how a crash begins.
Pray then to God that he forgive our sins.
The rain washes away and purifies.
Let it wash down the flesh we catered for.
And we who saw so much, and wanted more—
The crows will come and peck away our eyes.
Perhaps ambition used too sharp a goad
It drove us to these heights from which we swing
Hacked at by greedy starlings on the wing
Like horses' droppings on a country road.
Oh, brothers, learn from us how it begins
I pray that you kindly forgive our sins.

The men who break into your houses
Because they have no place to sleep in
The gossipper, the man who grouses
And likes to curse instead of weeping;
The women stealing your bread ration
Could be your mothers for two pins.
They're acting in too mild a fashion—
I pray you to forgive their sins.

Show understanding for their trouble
But none for those who, from high places
Led you to war and worse disgraces
And made you sleep on bloodstained rubble.
They plunged you into bloody robbery
And now they beg you to forgive.
So choke their mouths with the poor débris
That's left of where you used to live!

And those who think the whole thing's over
Saying 'Let them expiate their sins'
Are asking for a great iron crowbar
To stave their ugly faces in.

NEW CHORALE

Don't punish small wrong-doings too much. Never
Will they withstand the frost, for they are cold.

Think of the darkness and the bitter weather
The cries of pain that echo round this world.

But tackle the big crooks now, all together
And chop them down before you're all too old:
Who caused the darkness and the bitter weather
And brought the pain that echoes round this world.

['Anhang' to *The Threepenny Opera*, in GW *Stücke* 2, pp. 491 ff., excluding the 'Neufassung der Ballade vom angenehmen Leben', which differs only marginally from that in our text, and the closing verses from the film version, which we have given above (p. 84). The dates indicate that the first and fourth of these songs were written in 1948, the other two in 1946.]

ON *THE THREEPENNY OPERA*

Under the title *The Beggar's Opera, The Threepenny Opera* has been performed for the past two hundred years in theatres throughout England. It gives us an introduction to the life of London's criminal districts, Soho and Whitechapel, which are still the refuge of the poorest and least easily understood strata of English society just as they were two centuries ago.

Mr Jonathan Peachum has an ingenious way of capitalising on human misery by artificially equipping healthy individuals as cripples and sending them out to beg, thereby earning his profits from the compassion of the well-to-do. This activity in no sense results from inborn wickedness. 'My position in the world is one of self-defence' is Peachum's principle, and this stimulates him to the greatest decisiveness in all his dealings. He has but one serious adversary in the London criminal community, a gentlemanly young man called Macheath, whom the girls find divine. Macheath has abducted Peachum's daughter Polly and married her in highly eccentric fashion in a stable. On learning of his daughter's marriage—which offends him more on social grounds than on moral ones—Peachum launches an all-out war against Macheath and his gang of rogues; and it is the vicissitudes of this war that form the content of *The Threepenny Opera*. However, it ends with Macheath being saved literally from the gallows, and a grand, if somewhat parodistic operatic finale satisfactorily rounds it all off.

The Beggar's Opera was first performed in 1728 at the Lincoln's Inn Theatre. Contrary to what a number of German translators have supposed, its title does not signify an opera featuring beggars but 'the beggar's opera', in other words an opera for beggars. Written in response to a suggestion by the great Jonathan Swift, *The Beggar's Opera* was a parody of Handel, and it is said to have had a splendid result in that Handel's theatre became ruined. Since there is nowadays no target for parody on the scale of Handel's theatre all attempt at parody has been abandoned: the musical score is entirely modern. We still, however, have the same *sociological* situation. Just like two hundred years ago we have a social order in which virtually all levels, albeit in a wide variety of ways, pay respect to moral principles not by leading a moral life but by living off morality. Where its form is concerned, the *Threepenny Opera* represents a basic type of opera. It contains elements of opera and elements of the drama.

['Über die Dreigroschenoper—1' from GW *Schriften Zum Theater* p. 987. Dated 9 January 1929, when it appeared as an article in the *Augsburger Neueste Nachrichten* to introduce the production in Brecht's home town.]

NOTES TO *THE THREEPENNY OPERA*

The Reading of Plays

There is no reason why John Gay's motto for his *Beggar's Opera*—nos haec novimus esse nihil—should be changed for *The Threepenny Opera*. Its publication represents little more than the prompt-book of a play wholly surrendered to theatres, and thus is directed at the expert rather than at the consumer. This doesn't mean that the conversion of the maximum number of readers or spectators into experts is not thoroughly desirable; indeed it is under way.

The Threepenny Opera is concerned with bourgeois conceptions not only as content, by representing them, but also through the manner in which it does so. It is a kind of report on life as any member of the audience would like to see it. Since at the same time, however, he sees a good deal that he has no wish to see; since therefore he sees his wishes not merely fulfilled but also criticised (sees himself not as the subject but as the object), he is theoretically in a position to appoint a new function for the theatre. But the theatre itself resists any alteration of its function, and so it seems desirable that the spectator should read plays whose aim is not merely to be performed in the theatre but to change it: out of mistrust of the theatre.

Today we see the theatre being given absolute priority over the actual plays. The theatre apparatus's priority is a priority of means of production. This apparatus resists all conversion to other purposes, by taking any play which it encounters and immediately changing it so that it no longer represents a foreign body within the apparatus—except at those points where it neutralises itself. The necessity to stage the new drama correctly—which matters more for the theatre's sake than for the drama's—is modified by the fact that the theatre can stage anything: it theatres it all down. Of course this priority has economic reasons.

The Principal Characters

The character of JONATHAN PEACHUM is not to be resumed in the stereotyped formula 'miser'. He has no regard for money. Mistrusting as he does anything that might inspire hope, he sees money as just one more wholly ineffective weapon of defence. Certainly he is a rascal, a theatrical rascal of the old school. His crime lies in his conception of the world. Though it is a conception worthy in its ghastliness of standing alongside the achievements of any of the other great criminals, in making a commodity of human misery he is merely following the trend of the times. To give a practical example, when Peachum takes Filch's money in scene 1 he does not think of locking it in a cashbox but merely shoves it in his pocket: neither this nor any other money is going to save him. It is pure conscientiousness on his part, and a proof of his general despondency, if he does not just throw it away: he cannot throw away the least trifle. His attitude to a million shillings would be exactly the same. In his view neither his money (or all the money in the world) nor his head (or all the heads in the world) will see him through. And this is the reason why he never works but just wanders round his shop with his hat on his head and his hands in his pockets, checking that nothing is going astray. No truly worried man ever works. It is not meanness on his part if he has his Bible chained to his desk because he is scared someone might steal it. He never looks at his son-in-law before he has got him on the gallows, since no conceivable personal values of any kind could influence him to adopt a different approach to a man who deprives him of his daughter. Mac the Knife's other crimes only concern him in so far as they provide a means of getting rid of him. As for Peachum's daughter, she is like the Bible, just a potential aid. This is not so much repellent as disturbing, once you consider what depths of desperation are implied when nothing in the world is of any use except that minute portion which could help to save a drowning man.

The actress playing POLLY PEACHUM should study the foregoing description of Mr Peachum. She is his daughter.

The bandit MACHEATH must be played as a bourgeois phenomenon. The bourgeoisie's fascination with bandits rests on a misconception: that a bandit is not a bourgeois. This misconception is the child of another misconception: that a bourgeois is not a bandit. Does this mean that they are identical? No: occasionally a bandit is not a coward. The qualification 'peaceable' normally attributed to the bourgeois by our theatre is here achieved by Macheath's dislike, as a good businessman, of the shedding of blood except where strictly necessary—for the sake of the business. This reduction of bloodshed to a minimum, this economising, is a business principle; at a pinch Mr Macheath can wield an exceptionally agile blade. He is aware what is due to his legend: a certain romantic aura can further the economies in question if enough care is taken to spread it around. He is punctilious in ensuring that all hazardous, or at any rate bloodcurdling actions by his subordinates get ascribed to himself, and is just as reluctant as any professor to see his assistants put their name to a job. He impresses women less as a handsome man than as a well situated one. There are English drawings of *The Beggar's Opera* which show a short, stocky man of about forty with a head like a radish, a bit bald but not lacking dignity. He is emphatically staid, is without the least sense of humour, while his solid qualities can be gauged from the fact that he thinks more of exploiting his employees than of robbing strangers. With the forces of law and order he is on good terms; his common sense tells him that his own security is closely bound up with that of society. To Mr Macheath the kind of affront to public order with which Peachum menaces the police would be profoundly disturbing. Certainly his relations with the ladies of Turnbridge strike him as demanding justification, but this justification is adequately provided by the special nature of his business. Occasionally he has made use of their purely business relationship to cheer himself up, as any bachelor is entitled to do in moderation; but what he appreciates about this more private aspect is the fact that his regular and pedantically punctual visits to a certain Turnbridge coffee-house are *habits*, whose cultivation and proliferation is perhaps the main objective of his correspondingly bourgeois life.

In any case the actor playing Macheath must definitely not base his interpretation of the part on this frequenting of a disorderly house. It is one of the not uncommon but none the less incomprehensible instances of bourgeois demonism.

As for Macheath's true sexual needs, he naturally would rather satisfy them where he can get certain domestic comforts thrown in, in other words with women who are not entirely without means. He sees his marriage as an insurance for his business. However slight his regard for it, his profession necessitates a temporary absence from the capital, and his subordinates are highly unreliable. When he pictures his future he never for one moment sees himself on the gallows, just quietly fishing the stream on a property of his own.

BROWN the police commissioner is a very modern phenomenon. He is a twofold personality: his private and official natures differ completely. He lives not in spite of this fission but through it. And along with him the whole of society is living through its fission. As a private individual he would never dream of lending himself to what he considers his duty as an official. As a private individual he would not (and must not) hurt a fly. . . . In short, his affection for Macheath is entirely genuine; the fact that it brings certain business advantages does not render it suspect; too bad that life is always throwing mud at everything. . . .

Hints for actors

As for the communication of this material, the spectator must not be made to adopt the empathetic approach. There must be a process of exchange between spectator and actor, with the latter at bottom addressing himself directly to the spectator despite all the strangeness and detachment. The actor then has to tell the spectator more about his character 'than lies in the part'. He must naturally adopt the attitude which allows the episode to develop easily. At the same time he must also set up relationships with episodes other than those of the story, not just be the story's servant. In a love scene with Macheath, for instance, Polly is not only Macheath's beloved but also Peachum's daughter. Her relations with the spectator must embrace her criticisms of the accepted notions concerning bandits' women and shopkeepers' daughters.

1.* [p. 13] The actors should refrain from depicting these bandits as a collection of those depressing individuals with red neckerchiefs who frequent places of entertainment and with whom no decent person

*These figures refer to numbered passages in our text.

would drink a glass of beer. They are naturally sedate persons, some of them portly and all without exception good mixers when off duty.

2. [p. 13] This is where the actors can demonstrate the practical use of bourgeois virtues and the close relationship between dishonesty and sentiment.

3. [p. 14] It must be made clear how violently energetic a man needs to be if he is to create a situation in which a worthier attitude (that of a bridegroom) is possible.

4. [p. 17] What has to be shown here is the displaying of the bride, her fleshliness, at the moment of its final apportionment. At the very instant when supply must cease, demand has once again to be stimulated to its peak. The bride is desired all round; the bridegroom then sets the pace. It is, in other words, a thoroughly theatrical event. At the same time it has to be shown that the bride is hardly eating. How often one sees the daintiest creatures wolfing down entire chickens and fishes! Not so brides.

5. [p. 30] In showing such matters as Peachum's business the actors do not need to bother too much about the normal *development of the plot*. It is, however, important that they should present a development rather than an ambience. The actor playing one of the beggars should aim to show the selection of an appropriately effective wooden leg (trying on one, laying it aside, trying another, then going back to the first) in such a way that people decide to see the play a second time at the right moment to catch this turn; nor is there anything to prevent the theatre featuring it on the screens in the background.

6. [p. 38] It is absolutely essential that the spectator should see Miss Polly Peachum as a virtuous and agreeable girl. Having given evidence of her uncalculating love in the second scene, she now demonstrates that practical-mindedness which saves it from being mere ordinary frivolity.

7. [p. 42] These ladies are in undisturbed possession of their means of production. Just for this reason they must give no impression that they are free. Democracy for them does not represent the same freedom as it does for those whose means of production can be taken away from them.

8. [p. 45] This is where those Macheaths who seem least inhibited from portraying his death agony commonly baulk at singing the third verse. They would obviously not reject the sexual theme if a tragedy had been made of it. But in our day and age sexual themes undoubtedly belong in the realm of comedy; for sex life and social life conflict, and the resulting contradiction is comic because it can only be resolved historically, i.e. under a different social order. So

the actor must be able to put across a ballad like this in a comic way. It is very important how sexual life is represented on stage, if only because a certain primitive materialism always enters into it. The artificiality and transitoriness of all social superstructures becomes visible.

9. [p. 48] Like other ballades in *The Threepenny Opera* this one contains a few lines from François Villon in the German version by K. L. Ammer. The actor will find that it pays to read Ammer's translation, as it shows the differences between a ballade to be sung and a ballade to be read.

10. [p. 68] This scene is an optional one designed for those Pollys who have a gift for comedy.

11. [p. 73] As he paces round his cell the actor playing Macheath can at this point recapitulate all the ways of walking which he has so far shown the audience. The seducer's insolent way, the hunted man's nervous way, the arrogant way, the experienced way and so on. In the course of this brief stroll he can once again show every attitude adopted by Macheath in the course of these few days.

12. [p. 73] This is where the actor of the epic theatre is careful not to let his efforts to stress Macheath's fear of death and make it dominate the whole message of the Act, lead him to throw away the depiction of *true* friendship which follows. (True friendship is only true if it is kept within limits. The moral victory scored by Macheath's two truest friends is barely diminished by these two gentlemen's subsequent moral defeat, when they are not quick *enough* to hand over their means of existence in order to save their friend.)

13. [p. 76] Perhaps the actor can find some way of showing the following: Macheath quite rightly feels that in his case there has been a gruesome miscarriage of justice. And true enough, if justice were to lead to the victimisation of any more bandits than it does at present it would lose what little reputation it has.

About the singing of the songs

When an actor sings he undergoes a change of function. Nothing is more revolting than when the actor pretends not to notice that he has left the level of plain speech and started to sing. The three levels—plain speech, heightened speech and singing—must always remain distinct, and in no case should heightened speech represent an intensification of plain speech, or singing of heightened speech. In no case therefore should singing take place where words are prevented by excess of feeling. The actor must not only sing but show a man singing. His aim is not so much to bring out the emotional content of his song (has one the right to offer others a dish that one has already eaten one-self?) but to show gestures that are so to speak the habits and usage of the body. To this end he would be best advised not to use the actual words of the text when rehearsing, but common everyday phrases which express the same thing in the crude language of ordinary life. As for the melody, he must not follow it blindly: there is a kind of speaking-against-the-music which can have strong effects, the results of a stubborn, incorruptible sobriety which is independent of music and rhythm. If he drops into the melody it must be an event; the actor can emphasise it by plainly showing the pleasure which the melody gives him. It helps the actor if the musicians are visible during his perfor-mance and also if he is allowed to make visible preparation for it (by straightening a chair perhaps or making himself up, etc.). Particularly in the songs it is important that 'he who is showing should himself be shown'.

Why does the mounted messenger have to be mounted?

The Threepenny Opera provides a picture of bourgeois society, not just of 'elements of the Lumpenproletariat'. This society has in turn produced a bourgeois structure of the world, and thereby a specific view of the world without which it could scarcely hope to survive. There is no avoiding the sudden appearance of the Royal Mounted Messenger if the bourgeoisie is to see its own world depicted. Nor has Mr Peachum any other concern in exploiting society's bad conscience for gain. Workers in the theatre should reflect just why it is so particu-larly stupid to deprive the messenger of his *mount*, as nearly every modernistic director of the play has done. After all, if a judicial murder is to be shown, there is surely no better way of paying due tribute to the theatre's rôle in bourgeois society than to have the journalist who establishes the murdered man's innocence towed into court by a swan. Is it not a piece of self-evident tactlessness if people persuade the audi-ence to laugh at itself by making something comic of the mounted messenger's sudden appearance? Depriving bourgeois literature of the sudden appearance of some form of mounted messenger would reduce it to a mere depiction of conditions. The mounted messenger guaran-tees you a truly undisturbed appreciation of even the most intolerable conditions, so it is a *sine qua non* for a literature whose *sine qua non* is that it leads nowhere.

It goes without saying that the third finale must be played with total seriousness and utter dignity.

['Anmerkungen zur "Dreigroschenoper"', from GW *Schriften zum The-ater* p. 991 and *Stücke* p. 992, omitting paragraphs 2 ('Titles and screens') and 6 ('Why does Macheath have to be arrested twice over?'), which refer to Brecht's theatre as a whole rather than to this particular play. For these see *Brecht on Theatre*.]

Stage design for The Threepenny Opera

In *The Threepenny Opera* the more different the set's appearance as be-tween acting and songs, the better its design. For the Berlin production (1928) a great fairground organ was placed at the back of the stage, with steps on which the jazz band was lodged, together with coloured lamps that lit up when the orchestra was playing. Right and left of the organ were two big screens for the projection of Neher's drawings, framed in red satin. Each time there was a song its title was projected on them in big letters, and lights were lowered from the grid. So as to achieve the right blend of patina and newness, shabbiness and opu-lence, the curtain was a small, none too clean piece of calico running on metal wires. For the Paris production (1937) opulence and patina took over. There was a real satin drapery with gold fringes, above and to the side of which were suspended big fairground lamps which were lit during the songs. The curtain had two figures of beggars painted on it, more than life size, who pointed to the title 'The Threepenny Opera'. Screens with further painted figures of beggars were placed downstage right and left.

Peachum's beggars' outfitting shop

Peachum's shop must be so equipped that the audience is able to grasp the nature of this curious concern. The Paris production had two shop windows in the background containing dummies in beggars' outfits. Inside the shop was a stand from which garments and special headgear were suspended, all marked with white labels and numbers. A small low rack contained a few worn-out shoes, numbered like the garments, of a kind only seen in museums under glass. The Kamerny Theatre in Moscow showed Mr Peachum's clients entering the dress-ing booths as normal human beings, then leaving them as horrible wrecks.

['Aufbau der "Dreigroschenoper"-Bühne', from GW *Schriften zum The-ater* p. 1000. Dated c. 1937. Taïroff's production at the Kamerny Theatre in Moscow took place in 1930. The Paris designer was Eugène Berman.]

Note by Kurt Weill

ABOUT *THE THREEPENNY OPERA*
(A PUBLIC LETTER)

Thank you for your letter. I will be glad to say something about the course on which Brecht and I have embarked with this work, and which we mean to pursue further.

You speak of *The Threepenny Opera*'s sociological significance. True enough, the success of our play has shown this new genre not merely to have come at the right moment in terms of the artistic situation but also, apparently, to have responded to a positive longing on the public's part to see a favourite form of theatre revitalised. I doubt whether our form is going to replace operetta [. . .]. What really matters to all of us is the establishment of a first bridgehead in a consumer industry hitherto reserved for a very different category of writer and musician. *The Threepenny Opera* is putting us in touch with an audience which was previously ignorant of us, or at least would never have believed us capable of interesting a circle of listeners so much wider than the normal concert- and opera-going public.

Seen thus, *The Threepenny Opera* takes its place in a movement which today embraces nearly all the younger musicians. The abandonment of 'art for art's sake', the reaction against individualism in art, the ideas for film music, the link with the musical youth movement and, connecting with these, the simplification of musical means of expression—they are all stages along the same road.

Only opera remains stuck in its 'splendid isolation'. Its audiences continue to represent a distinct group of people seemingly outside the ordinary theatrical audience. Even today new operas incorporate a dramaturgical approach, a use of language, a choice of themes such as would be quite inconceivable in the modern theatre. And one is always hearing 'That's all very well for the theatre but it wouldn't do in opera.' Opera originated as an aristocratic branch of art, and everything labelled 'operatic tradition' goes to underline its basic social character. Nowadays, however, there is no other artistic form whose attitude is so undisguisedly social, the theatre in particular having switched conclusively to a line that can better be termed socially formative. If the operatic framework cannot stand such a comparison with the theatre of the times [*Zeittheater*], then that framework had better be broken up.

Seen in this light, nearly all the worthwhile operatic experiments of recent years emerge as basically destructive in character. *The Threepenny Opera* made it possible to start rebuilding, since it allowed us to go back to scratch. What we were setting out to create was the earliest form of opera. Every musical work for the stage raises the question: what on earth can music, and particularly singing, be doing in the theatre? In our case the answer was of the most primitive possible kind. I had before me a realistic plot, and this forced me to make the music work against it if I was to prevent it from making a realistic impact. Accordingly the plot was either interrupted, making way for music, or else deliberately brought to a point where there was no alternative but to sing. Furthermore it was a play that allowed us for once to take 'opera' as subject-matter for an evening in the theatre. At the outset the audience was told 'Tonight you are going to see an opera for beggars. Because this opera was so opulently conceived as only a beggar's imagination could make it, it is called *The Threepenny Opera*.' And so even the finale to the third Act is in no sense a parody, rather an instance of the very idea of 'opera' being used to resolve a conflict, i.e. being given a function in establishing the plot, and consequently having to be presented in its purest and most authentic form.

This return to a primitive operatic form entailed a drastic simplification of musical language. It meant writing a kind of music that would be singable by actors, in other words by musical amateurs. But if at first this looked like being a handicap, in time it proved immensely enriching. Nothing but the introduction of approachable, catchy tunes made possible *The Threepenny Opera*'s real achievement: the creation of a new type of musical theatre.

['Über die Dreigroschenoper' from Kurt Weill: *Ausgewählte Schriften*, ed. David Drew, Suhrkamp, Frankfurt 1975, p. 54. Originally published in

Anbruch, Vienna, January 1929, Jg. 11, Nr. 1, p. 24, where Weill was responding to a letter from the editors welcoming the success of a work which so accurately reflected contemporary social and artistic conditions, and asking for his theoretical views.]

Transcript

From a conversation between Brecht and Giorgio Strehler on 25 October 1955 with regard to the forthcoming Milan production. (Taken down by Hans-Joachim Bunge.)

Strehler had prepared twenty-seven precisely formulated questions for Brecht about the production of *The Threepenny Opera*. He began by asking its relation to the original *Beggar's Opera* and the extent of Elisabeth Hauptmann's and Kurt Weill's collaboration.

Brecht and Hauptmann told him that a play had been needed to open the Theater am Schiffbauerdamm under Fischer and Aufricht's direction on 28 August 1928. Brecht was engaged on *The Threepenny Opera*. It was based on a translation made by Elisabeth Hauptmann. The ensuing work with Weill and Elisabeth Hauptmann was a true collaboration and proceeded step by step. Erich Engel agreed to take over the direction. He had directed Brecht's early plays and Brecht had attended many of his rehearsals; he was the best man for an experiment like this. Perhaps the hardest thing was choosing the actors. Brecht went primarily for cabaret and revue performers, who had the advantage of being artistically interested and socially aggressive. During the summer Caspar Neher prepared his designs. According to Brecht the idea underlying *The Threepenny Opera* was: 'criminals are bourgeois: are bourgeois criminals?'.

Strehler asked whether there was any material about the first performance. He was convinced that 'Models' were useful and therefore needed it for his production. The sort of thing that would be of historical interest to him was to know the style of the production and the historical setting of the first performance. He asked if he was right in assuming that Brecht had shifted *The Threepenny Opera* to the Victorian era because of the latter's essentially bourgeois character, which meant that London rather than, say, Paris or Berlin provided the best setting. Brecht replied that from the outset he had wanted, primarily because of the shortage of time, to change the original as little as possible. Transporting it to Paris or some other city would have meant extensive changes in the portrayal of the setting, which in turn would have entailed much additional research. But even the best of principles couldn't be maintained indefinitely, and working on the play had led to the realisation that the original date could usefully be advanced a hundred years. A good deal was known about the Victorian age, which at the same time was remote enough to be judged with critical detachment, thus permitting the audience to pick out what was relevant to them. Set in that period the play would be more easily transported to Berlin than if set in that in which Gay had (of necessity) had to locate it.

Strehler observed that the music which Weill wrote in 1928 was of its own time and therefore evidently in deliberate contrast with the period of the play. Brecht said this was a gain for the theatre. The underlying thought was: beggars are poor people. They want to make a grand opera, but lack money and have to make do as best they can. How to show this? By a splendidly entertaining performance (which at the same time, of course, must lay bare the conditions prevailing at that period) and at the same time by making evident all that which failed to achieve the object intended, frequently indeed producing results actually opposed to it. For instance the beggar actors are quite unable to portray respectability (such as ought to be particularly easy in a Victorian setting), so that there are continual lapses, particularly in the songs. The grand manner at which they are aiming goes wrong, and suddenly it all turns into a dirty joke. This isn't what the beggar actors want, but the audience loves it and applauds, with the result that it all keeps slipping further into the gutter. They are alarmed by this, but all the same it works. Their plan to create a grand theatre proves impossible to realise. Because of their restricted means it only half comes off. (Here again the Victorian age gives the right picture.) In such a beggar's opera decency would be no inducement to the audience to stay in its seats; its preferences are accordingly respected. Only the finale has once again been carefully rehearsed, so that the level originally aimed at can at least be achieved here. Yet even this is a failure, for it succeeds only as parody. In short there is a perpetual effort to present something grandiose, but each time it is a fiasco. All the same a whole series of truths emerge.

Brecht gave an instance: unemployed actors trying to portray the Geneva conference. Unfortunately they have a quite wrong idea of it, and so with the best will in the world all their crocodile-like efforts to present Mr Dulles, for instance, as a Christian martyr are a failure, because they have no proper notion either of Mr Dulles or of a Christian martyr. Whatever they do is successful only in making people laugh. But to laugh is to criticise.

Strehler suggested that *The Beggar's Opera* was originally aristocratic in both form and content, a skit on Handel's operas for instance. Brecht had kept its form and its sense. All this was still valid in 1928. Capitalist society was still on its feet then, as was grand opera. Meantime there had been a war, but the problems had remained in many ways generally the same. Today however there were distinctions that must be made. Its relevance would still apply as forcefully in Italy and similar capitalist countries.

Brecht agreed. He thought the play ought to have the same power of attack in contemporary Italy as it had had at the time in Berlin.

Strehler asked how far was *The Threepenny Opera* an epic play and how epic ought the production to be.

Brecht emphasised that both considerations to a great extent applied. The socially critical stance must not be abandoned for a moment. The main prop here was the music, which kept on destroying the illusion; the latter, however, had first to be created, since an atmosphere could never be destroyed until it had been built up.

Strehler expressed regret that so many *Threepenny Opera* productions had been prettified. Not that its socially critical aspects could be entirely camouflaged, but it had remained a nice theatrical revolution which failed to get across the footlights, not unlike those lions that can be safely visited in zoos, where you are protected from attacks by iron bars. The average director made concessions to his audience, and it wasn't going to pay 2,000 lire to have filth thrown at it. The way *The Threepenny Opera* was normally performed, like an elegant Parisian opera, everybody found it 'nice'.

Brecht explained that when *The Threepenny Opera* was originally staged in Germany in 1928 it had a strong political and aesthetic impact. Among its successful results were:

1. The fact that young proletarians suddenly came to the theatre, in some cases for the first time, and then quite often came back.
2. The fact that the top stratum of the bourgeoisie was made to laugh at its own absurdity. Having once laughed at certain attitudes, it would never again be possible for these particular representatives of the bourgeoisie to adopt them.

The Threepenny Opera can still fulfil the same function in capitalist countries today so long as people understand how to provide entertainment and, at the same time, bite instead of mere cosy absurdity. The important point now being: look, beggars are being fitted out. Every beggar is a monstrosity. The audience must be appalled at its own complicity in such poverty and wretchedness.

Strehler asked if Brecht could suggest any ways of ensuring that *The Threepenny Opera* should be as artistically effective and topically relevant in 1955 as in 1928. Brecht replied that he would heighten the crooks' make-up and render it more unpleasant. The romantic songs must be sung as beautifully as possible, but the falsity of this 'attempt at a romantic island where everything in the garden is lovely' needed to be strongly underlined.

Strehler was anxious to get material about the set, but what his Milan production most needed was some suggestions about costumes, since he felt that the 1928 costumes, which so far as he knew were based wholly on the Victorian era, would no longer be of use to him. Brecht corrected him, saying that far from being Victorian the 1928 costumes had been gathered from the costumiers and were a complete mixture. He would not think of abandoning the use of rhyme as in *The Beggar's Opera*, nor, with it, the 'jazzed up Victorianism' of the Berlin production. In the Moscow production Taïroff had entirely modernised the costumes so as to conjure up the (by Moscow standards) exotic appeal of Paris fashions.

Brecht said that Strehler had the right picture: up went the curtain on a brothel, but it was an utterly bourgeois brothel. In the brothel there were whores, but there was no mystique about them, they were utterly bourgeois whores. Everything is done to make things proper and lawful.

Strehler asked how far *The Threepenny Opera* was a satire on grand opera, to which Brecht replied: only in so far as grand opera still persists, but that this had never been so important in Germany as in Italy. The starting point must always be a poor theatre trying to do its best.

Strehler asked what did Brecht think about adaptation to bring it up to date. Brecht thought such a procedure acceptable. Strehler's question sprang from the fact that it would be impossible, for instance, to stage *The Threepenny Opera* in Naples using Kurt Weill's music. However, in Milan there were parallels with the reign of Umberto I which would be brought out. To this extent Milan was comparable with London, while the popular note struck by the music would have the same reception as in Berlin. The bourgeoisie was the same. But Strehler wondered if the need to Italianise the names might not eliminate the necessary critical detachment: for 'one must bare one's teeth for the truth'.

Brecht wondered if it might not be possible to set *The Threepenny Opera* in the Italian quarter of New York around 1900 perhaps. The music would be right too. He had not gone into the question as yet but at the moment he thought it a possible transposition. The New York Italians had brought everything, including their emotions, from back home, but it had all got commercialised. There would be a brothel, but one like at home, to which they'd go because they felt it was 'like being back at mamma's'.

Strehler took this idea further and asked if it wouldn't mean adding a prologue. Here again Brecht agreed, in so far as some explanation would be needed. It would have to be established that the New York beggar actors were a group of Italians, that it was all like in Milan but a long way off. The first skyscrapers could have been built, but the group must be wretchedly poor. All they want to do is to stage something 'like back home'.

Strehler had a suggestion for the prologue. A film of Milan could be shown, leading the actors to want to perform something recalling that city, whereupon the curtain would rise and the play begin.

Another reservation of Strehler's concerned the Italian actor's penchant for improvisation. 'You send someone off to choose a costume and he comes back with fifty.' There was also the problem of 'the epic style of portrayal'. According to Strehler it is not easy for the Italian actor to play on more than one level at a time, i.e. roughly to the effect that 'I am acting a man trying to act this character.' He asked if it was at all possible to perform Brecht's plays—e.g. *The Mother*, which he described as the 'stronghold of the epic theatre'—except in an epic manner, and where if anywhere they could be performed if one had no actors or directors who had been trained for them. 'What is the result of acting them in the wrong way?' Brecht: 'They can certainly be performed, but what emerges is normal theatre, and three-quarters of the fun is lost.'

Strehler wanted some advice about what to do with actors who knew nothing about epic theatre. He asked if it was possible to perform a Brecht play given only *one* actor familiar with the epic theatre, and he inquired about methods for teaching the epic way of acting.

Brecht told Strehler not to worry and that our own acting too was only partly epic. It always worked best in comedies, since they anyway entail a measure of alienation. The epic style of portrayal was more easily achieved there, so that it was a good idea generally to stage plays more or less as comedies. He suggested using an aid which he had tried himself: having the actors intersperse what he called 'bridge verses', thus turning their speech into a report in indirect speech; i.e.

interspersing the sentences with 'said he's. 'What's bad is that "epic" cannot be achieved without using the dialectic.'

Strehler said he was convinced that nowadays it was impossible to act either Shakespeare or the earlier tragedies without alienation if their performance was to be useful and entertaining.

Brecht once again suggested acting tragic scenes for their comic effect. What is most epic, he maintained, is always the run-throughs, and they should certainly be scheduled for the end of the rehearsals or better still conducted at regular intervals throughout the whole rehearsal period. 'The nearer the performance gets to being a run-through, the more epic it will be.' Strehler asked if his way of explaining epic portrayal to his actors was the right one, when he would cite the example of a director acting a scene, showing the actors in outline how to do something and all the time having his explanations ready even if he never voices them. Brecht approved of this and thought that the actors too could be put in the director's situation if one instituted run-throughs with minimal use of gesture, so that everyone simply noted how things should go.

Strehler feared that his *Threepenny Opera* production might turn out 'neither fish nor fowl'. His sense of responsibility had held him back from doing *Mother Courage*, since he was unable to find an epic actress to play the title part. This production of *The Threepenny Opera* too was something that he had been planning for years and always had to put off because of a shortage of suitable actors.

['Über eine Neuinszenierung der Dreigroschenoper', from *Bertolt Brechts Dreigroschenbuch* (Suhrkamp, Frankfurt 1960) pp. 130–134. Strehler's production for the Piccolo Teatro, Milan, in 1957 eventually transposed the play to an American setting around the time of the First World War, with the police as Keystone Cops and an early motor car on stage. Brecht and Elisabeth Hauptmann thought it excellent.

At the Geneva Conference of summer 1954 the Western powers, China and the Soviet Union agreed to create two Vietnams, North and South. John Foster Dulles was then U.S. Secretary of State. King Umberto I's reign in Italy was from 1878 to 1900.]

Editorial Notes

1. GENERAL

Though there is little in the way of manuscript material or notes to show just how it evolved, *The Threepenny Opera* was clearly one of Brecht's more rapidly written works. Its producer Aufricht only took over the Theater am Schiffbauerdamm at the end of 1927, and it must have been in March or April 1928 that he and his dramaturg Heinrich Fischer went to Brecht in search of a play. What Brecht then offered them—apparently as his own work and under the title *Gesindel* or *Scum*—was a translation of *The Beggar's Opera* which Elisabeth Hauptmann had almost completed; he is said to have shown them the first two scenes. Nothing of this first script has come down to us, and there is no real evidence that Brecht himself had as yet taken any hand in it. The process of 'adaptation' credited to him by the original programme probably only started once the play itself and the principle of a collaboration with Weill had been accepted. Erich Engel, with whom Brecht had been working on the Berlin *Man equals Man*, was already earmarked as the play's director.

The next event seems to have been the production of a stage script which was duplicated by Brecht's and Hauptmann's agents, Felix Bloch Erben, and presumably represented the work done by the collaborators in the south of France that summer. Its title is given as 'The Beggar's Opera / Die Luden-Oper [The Ragamuffins' Opera] / translated by Elisabeth Hauptmann / German adaptation: Bert Brecht. Music: Kurt Weill'. Though its text is still a good way from the final version it already represents a considerable transformation of the original. Several subsequently discarded characters from Gay's original still remain (notably Mrs Coaxer and her girls), but Lockit has already been purged, together with all that part of the plot involving him, and replaced by the rather more up-to-date figure of Brown. Peachum's

manipulation of the beggars is also new, as are the first stable and second gaol scenes. The main items retained from Gay in this script are,
in our present numbering, scenes 1, 3, 4, 5 (which is not yet a brothel
but a room in the hotel), 6, 8 and the principle of the artificial happy
ending. There are no scene titles. However, Macheath's final speech
before his execution is already there, much as in our version, as are
several of the songs: Peachum's Morning Hymn (whose melody is in
fact a survivor from the original, being that of Gay's opening song),
Pirate Jenny, the Cannon Song, the Barbara Song, the Tango-Ballade,
the Jealousy Duet, Lucy's subsequently cut aria (in scene 8), the Call
from the Grave and the Ballad in which Macheath Begs All Men for
Forgiveness; also the final chorus. Most of these are not given in full,
but only by their titles, and some may not yet have been completed.
There are also two of Gay's original songs, as well as two translations
from Kipling: 'The Ladies' and 'Mary, Pity Women'. Neither the Gay
nor the Kipling songs were, so far as anybody knows, set by Weill, but
but the latter may explain why the original programme spoke of 'interpolated songs . . . by Rudyard Kipling'.

   This script was altered and added to in the course of the rehearsals,
when texts of several of the songs were stuck in and the rest added.
The piano score, which includes all the present songs apart from the
Ballad of Sexual Obsession, was published not long after the première, the text in Brecht's *Versuche 3* only in 1931. This 1931 text
has remained virtually unaltered, though Brecht appended a certain
amount of alternative material later, and is to all intents and purposes
that used for our translation.

2. THE 1928 STAGE SCRIPT

Act One

Scene 1

The dramatis personae originally included Gay's Mrs Coaxer and Suky
Tawdry; Jenny was Jenny Diver, as in Gay, which Brecht later rendered
'Spelunken-Jenny' or literally 'Low Den Jenny', perhaps on the assump-
tion that 'Diver' meant a habituée of dives. The script starts the play
without any scene title and with the following stage directions:

*Mr Peachum's house. It is 7 am. Peachum is standing at a desk on which
lie a ledger and a Bible. Round the walls are notices with such sayings as
'Give and it shall be given unto you', 'Close not thine ear to misery', 'You*

will benefit from the interests of a powerful organisation' and *'If you are satisfied tell the others, if you are dissatisfied tell me'.*

Peachum sings his Morning Hymn, then:

So. Now, one glance at the Bible and then to work. Matthew 5. I'm always combing Matthew for something I can use. No good. I'll have to cut it out once and for all. Salt without an egg. Matthew 6: feeble, feeble. No personality there. Wait. Verse 25: Give and it shall be given unto you. Flat, but it's been used already. Proverbs is still the best, particularly chapter 6. All kinds of useful lessons, if a bit old-fashioned. Yes, a business man like me, Robert Jeremiah Peachum and Co., who's forced to live among thieves, whores and lawyers, cannot do without God. Or let's say, without God and accountancy. We must add to that application, seriousness, circumspection, genius and economy. Not to mention early rising and kindness and loyalty . . .

This leads to Filch's entrance, after which the dialogue continues much as now up to the production of outfit C (p. 8). There is then no showcase with wax dummies; instead Mrs Peachum *'drags out a box full of indescribably ragged clothes'.* Instead of Peachum's speech exhibiting the various outfits Filch is simply told to 'Take off your clothes' etc. (p. 9), and these then become outfit A, the young man who has seen better days.

Filch removes his socks under protest (p. 9), and then as Mrs Peachum brings in the screen Peachum asks, much as in Gay's scene 4:

Did that fellow Macheath come round yesterday? The one who's always coming when I'm out?

MRS PEACHUM: Certainly, Bobby dear. There's no finer gentleman. If he comes from the Cuttlefish Bar at any reasonable hour we're going to a little hop with him—the Captain, Polly, Bob the Saw and me. Bobby, my Dear, is the Captain rich?

The dialogue remains close to Gay's (which we will make identifiable by its use of capital letters for nouns, as in German), down to Mrs Peachum's statement of her concern about Polly (which comes just before her first song in *The Beggar's Opera*). Then Filch appears in his new begging outfit and asks for a few tips (p. 11).

PEACHUM *inspects him, then to Mrs Peachum:* Half-wit? Yes, that'll be the best thing. *To Filch:* Nobody stupid can play the half-wit, you know. Come back this evening . . .

etc. (which is not in Gay). But after his 'Fifty per cent!' Peachum says
'To come back to Polly . . .' and returns to a cross between Gay's text
and ours. Thus:

> A handsome Wench in our way of Business is as profitable as at the Bar
> of a *Temple* Coffee-House. You should try to influence the girl in the
> right direction. In any thing but Marriage! After that, my Dear, how
> shall we be safe? You must imagine we can live on air. The way you
> chuck your daughter around anyone would think I'm a millionaire. The
> fellow would have us in his clutches in three shakes. In his clutches! Do
> you think your daughter can hold her tongue in bed any better than you?
> *Polly* is Tinder, and a Spark will at once set her on a Flame. Married! All
> she can think about is her own Pleasure, not her own Profit. Do you sup-
> pose we nurtured her at our breast . . . ?
>
> MRS PEACHUM: Our?
>
> PEACHUM: All right, you nurtured her; but did you nurture her so we
>   should have no crust to eat in our old age? Married! I expect my
>   daughter to be to me as bread to the hungry—*He leafs through the
>   book.*—it even says so in the Bible somewhere. Anyway marriage is dis-
>   gusting. I'll teach her to get married.
>
> MRS PEACHUM: Dear Bobby, you're just a barbarian. You're being unfair
>   to her. She is doing exactly what any decent girl would do: a few Liber-
>   ties for the Captain in the interest of the business.
>
> PEACHUM: But 'tis your Duty, my Dear, as her mother, to explain to the
>   girl what she owes to herself, or to us, which amounts to the same
>   thing. I'll go to her this moment and sift her.

At this point, corresponding to the end of Gay's scene 4, Peachum
moves on to what became part of his long speech on p. 9, the com-
plaints of client no. 136, then goes out telling Mrs Peachum to get on
with ironing in the wax. Left alone, as in Gay's scene 5, she says:

> God, was Bobby worked up! I can't say I blame him, though; I can't say I
> blame him.

Peachum returns, and the final exchanges are as in our text, less the song.

Scene 2

Again there is no title (this applies throughout the stage script), but the
stage direction says '*Empty stable. 5 pm the next day. It is fairly dark.
Enter Macheath with Matt of the Mint and Polly.*' There is nothing in
Gay corresponding to this scene.

The dialogue starts as in our text, roughly as far as Ned's 'Dear Polly' (p. 14), though without the lines in which Macheath shows his ignorance of Peachum. After Ned says this Mac, having knocked his hat off, *'shoves him against the wall, pushing his face with the flat of his hand—a favourite manoeuvre'*. Thence it continues as now down to Polly's inquiry 'Was the whole lot stolen?' (p. 15).

> MACHEATH: Stolen? Selected! Anybody can steal, and everybody does. But selecting the right items . . . That's where art comes in. What incompetence! [etc. as now, p. 15].

Thereafter the dialogue is much as now down to Jimmy's 'Hey, Captain, the cops!' (p. 19), though there is no mention of Jenny Diver by Jake (p. 17). Jimmy's exclamation this time heralds Brown's entrance, not that of the Rev. Kimball (who does not appear at all), and it turns out it is Brown's prospective son-in-law the Duke of Devonshire who is the stable's owner: 'Did it have to be Teddy's stable?' says Brown. 'At this of all times?' Mac welcomes him with 'Sit down, you old bugger and pitch into the egg mayonnaise' (cf. p. 23). He observes the origins of the plates and the eggs, then listens to the gang sing 'Bill Lawgen' (which is not from the original) and comments on the salmon:

> Clark's, the fishmongers. Breaking and entering reported this morning. Tastes delicious.

This is where Polly performs 'Pirate Jenny', which provokes the same reactions as in our text, apart from its references to Rev. Kimball. After 'let's not have any more of it' (p. 22) Mac goes straight on with 'You have today in your midst . . .' (p. 23), the speech leading into the Cannon Song. Only the title of this is given, but its first version had already been written some years earlier and published in the *Devotions for the Home* under the title 'Song of the Three Soldiers'; it is sometimes, on no clear grounds, described as 'after Kipling'.

After the song the text is much as now down to Brown's 'There's nothing whatsoever on record against you at Scotland Yard' (p. 25), apart from the interpolation at the end of Macheath's long speech (p. 25) of 'Cheers, Brown! And now for some music!'—at which *'Everything is cleared to one side. Three of the guests take it in turns to form a little jazz band.'* This prepares the way for the dance which concludes the scene. During it Macheath stands in the centre and says:

My dear friends. Let us bring this day to a worthy conclusion by con-
ducting ourselves as gentlemen.

WALTER *dancing with Polly:* Oh, stuff this day.

After which '*The party continues in full swing. Once again we hear the
chorus "Bill Lawgen and Mary Syer"* '—i.e. not the present Love Duet.

Scene 3

This starts close to Gay's scene 6, with indications of some intimacy
between Mrs Peachum and Filch:

> *Mr Peachum's office. Morning. Mrs Peachum. Filch.*
>
> MRS PEACHUM: Come hither, *Filch.* I am as fond of this Child, as though
> my Mind misgave me he were my own. Why are you so sad? Can your
> mamma not help?
>
> FILCH *tonelessly:* Oh dear, I can't regard you as my mamma, Mrs
> Peachum, even though I shouldn't say it.

He says how hard it is to beg, and regrets his choice of profession. She
wants him to find out about Macheath and Polly, who has now been
away from home for three days. Filch knows, but as in Gay has promised not to tell:

> MRS PEACHUM: Right, Filch, you shall go with me into my own Room,
> Filch. You shall tell me the whole Story in comfort, Filchy, and I'll give
> thee a Glass of Cordial Médoc that I keep locked up in my bedside
> table for my own drinking. *Exeunt.*

Peachum enters with Polly, and Gay's scene 7 follows, including Polly's
song 'Virgins are like the fair Flower', whose text is translated in toto.
Mrs Peachum then appears, but without her song from the original,
and goes straight into her opening speech of the scene in our version.
A shortened version of Gay's scene 8 dialogue follows, down to where
Peachum pinches Polly, asking 'Are you really bound Wife to him, or
are you only upon liking?'; he forbids Macheath the house, and Polly
(in lieu of 'Can Love be control'd by Advice?') goes into the Barbara
Song (which expands and updates the same theme, and whose text is
given in full). Mrs Peachum's faint (p. 29) then follows much as in Gay,
though now she asks for the Cordial and doubts Polly's 'Readiness and
Concern'.

Only one beggar then enters, who proves to be the disgruntled no.
136. 'First-class stains, Mr Twantry,' says Polly, handing over the
criticised outfit. The problem now, as in Gay's scene 10, is: how is

Polly to live. Peachum answers 'It's all perfectly simple' etc. as now (p. 31), and Polly's refusal to consider divorce follows. Then back, more or less, to Gay:

> PEACHUM: Yes, yes, yes. You're a silly little goose. But it's all so simple. You secure what he's got; I get him hanged at the next Sessions, and then at once you are made a charming Widow.
> POLLY: What, murder the Man I love! The Blood runs cold at my Heart with the very thought of it. But it would be murder!
> PEACHUM: Murder? Rubbish. Self-defence. It's all self-defence. My position in the world is one of self-defence.

—this last, crucial idea being new. Mrs Peachum then reminds Polly of her filial duties, as in Gay, and refers to 'Those cursed Play-Books she reads' before threatening to 'tan her behind' (p. 31). Peachum's last word is 'Polly, you will get a divorce!'

The rest of the scene is not in Gay. It strikes eleven, and a crowd of beggars streams in—'The second shift,' says Peachum. They arrive decently dressed, but change into their begging outfits, stumps, bandages etc. This introduces the present dialogue from the speech of complaint on p. 30 down to 'This one will do,' with the addition of a tirade by Peachum against his daughter. Mrs Peachum's speech 'Anyway, he's got several women' (p. 31) follows, after which the dialogue continues much as ours down to Polly's 'There's nothing on record against Mac at Scotland Yard' (p. 32):

> PEACHUM: Right. Then put on your hat, and we will go to Mr Brown. *To his wife:* And you'll go to Turnbridge. For the villainy of the world is great, and a man needs to run his legs off to keep them from being stolen from under him.
> POLLY: I, Papa, shall be delighted to shake hands with Mr Brown again.

But in lieu of the First Act finale, Polly then sings a translation of Gay's song against lawyers, 'A Fox may steal your Hens, Sir'.

Act Two

Scene 4 [1 in script]

This is set as '*Stable. Morning. Macheath. Enter Walter.*' The two men start with a version of the Peachum—Filch dialogue from Gay's Act 1, scene 2. Black Moll becomes 'Blattern-Molly' [Pockmarked Molly], who can be 'back on the beat tomorrow', says Macheath.

Betty Sly is 'Betriebs-Betty' [Busy Betty]. Tom Gagg is unchanged.
After Gay's line 'There is nothing to be got by the Death of Women,
except our Wives' Walter (not Filch) is sent with a message to Newgate, having first been told to look through the storeroom to see if
there are any decent clothes. Mrs Trapes needs them 'to clothe five
young pigeons to work Kensington Street'. On his exit Polly enters as
at the start of our scene, whose opening dialogue approximately follows, as far as the entry of the gang (p. 38). Once again, the listing of
the gang members (p. 37) derives from Peachum's speech in Act 1
scene 3 of the original, and includes such figures as Harry Padding-
ton, Slippery Sam ('Schleicher-Samuel') and Tom Tipple ('Tippel-
Tom'). The poetic naming of 'Bob the Pickpocket alias Gorgon alias
Bluff-Robert alias Carbuncle alias Robert the Saw' is mainly from
Gay, but Brecht makes him the gang member Polly likes best. The
speech about Jack Poole and banking is not in the script; the list simply ends, and Polly says her 'Why, Mac!' etc. as on p. 38, to introduce
the gang's entry.

Their first exchanges are somewhat different, to where Mac tells
them of his 'little trip' (p. 38). He and they then go into the storeroom
while Polly delivers a monologue; there is no demonstration of her
authority over the gang. They re-enter, and Mac resumes 'The rotten
part of it is' etc. (p. 39) down to 'toffs are all drunk'. Robert follows
with 'Ma'am, while your husband is away', etc.; Polly says 'goodbye,
Mr Robert' and shakes hands; then they leave as on page 40. Her dialogue with Macheath follows as now, as far as 'Highgate Heath'
(middle of page):

> POLLY: Then everything is all right. Goodbye, Mac.
> MAC: Goodbye, Polly. *He shuts the door behind her. Lighting a pipe:* Polly
> is most confoundedly bit. Now I must have Women. There is nothing
> unbends the Mind like them. Cocktails are not nearly such a help.

—the last sentence being Brecht's gloss on Gay's lines. He then opens
the storeroom door and tells Walter to assemble the Drury Lane ladies
for him at 8 pm in Room 5 of the Cuttlefish Hotel (equivalent to the
Tavern near Newgate of Gay's Act 2).

> MAC: Hurry! *Exit Walter.* This London owes me something for having
> fixed it up with a capital lot of women.

He speaks the final rhymed couplet, which our text gives to Polly, and
there is no Interlude.

Scene 5 *[2 in script]*

Cuttlefish Hotel. 8 pm. Room 5. Mac and Walter.
MACHEATH *rings.*
WALTER: Captain?
MAC: How long am I to wait for the ladies?
WALTER: They're bound to be here soon.

Macheath then sings 'The Ballad of the Ladies', translated from Kipling (and now included in GW *Gedichte* p. 1052). The bell rings again, and they troop in, the complete party from Gay's Act 2 scene 4: Mrs Coaxer, Dolly Trull, Mrs Vixen, Betty Doxy, Jenny Diver, Mrs Slammekin, Suky Tawdry and Molly Brazen, with Walter bringing up the rear. Macheath makes approximately the same speech of welcome as there, down to where the music strikes up 'the *French* Tune', i.e. the Cotillon. Molly: 'Ach, cash makes you randy' (a phrase of Brecht's which comes in others of his plays); then in lieu of the Cotillon the ladies *'dance a little "Step"'*, and Gay's dialogue follows, down to Mrs Vixen's 'to think too well of your friends'. Mac interrupts it with his 'Nice underwear you've got there, Vixen,' introducing our present dialogue down to Second Whore's 'I just don't wear any' (p. 44). Gay takes over again with the exchange between Mac and Jenny, which leads, however, not to her 'Before the Barn-Door crowing' song but to 'the brothel-ballade by François Villon', as yet without its text. The hand-reading episode follows as in our text from Dolly's first line down to Mac's 'Go on!' (p. 43), after which Jenny says she cannot do so, and then disarms him, aided as in Gay by Suky Tawdry. It is, however, Mrs, not Mr Peachum who enters with the constables, and she then makes very much the Peachum speech from Act 2 scene 5 of the original. Walter, who has been sitting reading, runs out like Jake in our text, and all exeunt *'most ceremoniously'*.

Scene 6 *[3 in script]*

This is described as *'Prison in Newgate. Brown sitting impatiently in a cell'*. The scene begins as in our text, down to Brown's exit (p. 47). Gay's Act 2 scene 7 then follows, with Smith filling Lockit's rôle. Left alone, Macheath makes his speech 'That miserable Brown . . .' as in our text (p. 47), but instead of the exchange with Smith he then continues 'But the worst of it . . .' (p. 48) as far as 'into a tiger', after which he goes on much as in Gay's scene 8:

I shall have a fine time on't betwixt this and my Execution. Here must I (all Day long) be confin'd to hear the Reproaches of a Wench who lays her

Ruin at my Door—just when a prisoner has some right at least to peace
and solitude. But here she comes: Lucy, and I cannot get from her. Wou'd
I were deaf!

Lucy enters and upbraids Macheath, as in Gay's scene 9, whose dialogue is then approximately followed, omitting the three songs, down to
the end of that scene: Lucy's cry 'O Mac, I only want to become an honest woman,' as in our text (p. 50). After that she *sings the song "Maria,
Fürsprecherin der Frauen"* ', i.e. Kipling's 'Mary, Pity Women', whose
translation follows in full, and is also given in GW *Gedichte* p. 1055.

The next section is not in Gay: Lucy continues 'Oh, Macheath, I do
hope you will lift my troubles from my shoulders.'

> MAC: Of course. As I said: as soon as I'm master of my own decisions.
> LUCY: But how are you going to get free? My father truly was your best
> friend, and even if you played a dirty trick on him over me he can't re-
> alise it. So what is he after you for?
> MAC: Don't talk to me about your father.
> LUCY: But I just don't understand what could have led him to put you in
> irons. There's some secret involving Peachum and his making such an
> awful threat that Daddy fainted on hearing it.
> MAC: If that's so it's all up with me.
> LUCY: No, no, you must become master of your decisions. My whole life
> depends on it. You must do all right, Mac. You'll end up all right, Mac.

Polly then appears as in Gay's Act 2 scene 13 (p. 50), his dialogue being followed approximately as far as the song 'How happy could I be
with either?' Instead of this song, however, *'Polly and Lucy sing
"Come on out, you Rose of Old Soho"* ' (whose title only is given, and
which could well relate also to the next song 'I am bubbled, I'm bubbled, O how I am troubled'). Then Gay's dialogue is resumed as far as
Peachum's entrance at the end of the scene, but prolonging the
Polly–Lucy dialogue as in our text from Lucy's 'What's that? What's
that?' (p. 53) to Mac's 'Polly!'. Peachum's entrance is then replaced by
that of Mrs Peachum, who drags Polly off much as he did in Gay's
scene 14, after which scene 15 is followed for much of the exchanges
between Macheath and Lucy, down to her 'It's wonderful the way you
say that. Say it again' (p. 55). On his saying that she must help him she
embroiders Gay's original thus:

If only I knew what was the matter with my father. Anyway the constables
are all drunk and it's the coronation tomorrow and my father sent someone

out for fifteen bottles of gin and when he didn't come back at once his wor-
ries overcame him and he upped and drank a whole bottle of the house-
keeper's scent. Now he's lying drunk as a lord beside his desk muttering
'Mackie!' If I can find the key shall I escape with you, darling?

They leave together as at the end of Gay's Act. Then a new concluding
episode follows, starting with a '*gentle knock*' and Brown's voice calling 'Mac!' (p. 55). Peachum appears much as in our text, though without his opening remarks to Smith, and our dialogue follows as far as
his 'People are sure to say . . . that the police shouldn't have let him escape' (p. 56). He rounds off this speech with 'A pity: the coronation
might have passed off without a single ugly incident.'

BROWN: What is that supposed to mean?
PEACHUM: That as it is the poorest of the poor won't let themselves be
    done out of attending the coronation tomorrow morning.
BROWN: What do you mean by the poorest of the poor?
PEACHUM: It is reasonable to assume that I mean beggars. You see, it is like
    this. These poorest of the poor—give and it shall be given unto you, and
    so on—have nothing in the world apart from celebrations. Well, there
    are various possibilities. Of course there has to be a criminal. What hap-
    pens to him is less important. Either they want to see a murderer hanged
    or they want to see one crowned. All the rest is immaterial.
BROWN: Look here, Mr Peachum, what do you mean by a murderer being
    crowned?
PEACHUM: Same as you do, Mr Brown.
BROWN: That's outrageous.
PEACHUM: Quite right, that's outrageous.
BROWN: You have given yourself away, Peachum. Hey, Smith!
PEACHUM: Don't bring him into this. Or I'll be awkward. There'll be a
    lot happening tomorrow morning. The papers will report how in the
    morning fog an unusual number of poor people of all kinds could be
    observed in the twisting alleys, patriots all of them with joyous faces
    and little signs round their necks: 'I gave my leg for the king', or 'My
    arm lies on Clondermell Field', or 'Three cheers for the king; the
    Royal Artillery made me deaf'. And all these patriots with just one ob-
    jective, the streets the coronation procession will take. *Drily:* Of
    course any of these people would much prefer, just supposing there
    could be an execution of a really well-known and reasonably popular
    murderer around the same hour, to attend that, as it is always more
    agreeable to see murderers hanged than crowned. Your servant,
    Brown. *Exit.*

BROWN: Now only the mailed fist can help. Sergeants! Report to me at the double!

There is no Second Act finale in the script.

Act Three
Scene 7 [1 in script]

The setting is 'Peachum's Beggars' Outfitting Shop. 5 am', and a Salvation Army hymn is being played off. Beggars are dressing. Great activity. Peachum is not on, so his opening remark (of our text) occurs later. Otherwise the dialogue is close to ours as far as Brown's entrance (p. 62), except that the Ballad of Sexual Obsession is not included, nor the dialogue following it down to Mrs Peachum's appearance with the tray (p. 62). Instead there is an exchange between a phony cripple and an authentic one. When Brown enters he 'appears to have been transformed into a tiger', and goes round 'spreading alarm like a great beast of prey'. His big opening speech starting 'Here we are. And now, Mr Beggar's Friend' (p. 62) goes on:

> In the very earliest times—listen, now just you think about it—humanity understood the idea of friendship. Even the most bestial examples—look carefully—felt the urge to acquire a friend. And whatever they may have done in that grey prehistoric age they stood by their comrades. Thigh to thigh they sat in danger, arm in arm they went through this vale of tears, and whatever they grabbed they shared, man to man: think about it. And that is what I feel too, just as I've described it. I too, despite all weakness and temptation place a value on friendship, and I too . . .
> PEACHUM: Good morning, Brown, good morning.

The speech echoes Brecht's early 'Ballad of Friendship' (*Poems 1913–1956*, p. 52), and after it the dialogue remains close to ours from Peachum's remark (p. 62) to his 'You see, Brown' (p. 64) immediately before the music, though omitting the ten lines before the drum-roll. Then he goes on to tell Brown that the beggars are fakes, just a few young people dressing up to celebrate having a king once more, and concludes 'I've nothing against it; it was quite *harmless*.' When no sound follows he repeats this remark. Then 'a kind of band is heard playing an excruciating "Step"'.

BROWN: What's that?
PEACHUM: Dance music.

> *Beggars and whores 'steppen'* [*dance a 'step'*].
PEACHUM: Take off those chains, Smith. Yes, this is how the poor enjoy themselves . . .

He goes up to Brown and says:

> As for you, Brown, your situation is no laughing matter. This is a little dance, but in Drury Lane it is bloody serious. You see, there are so many poor people. Thousands of them. When you see them standing outside the Abbey . . .

and so on, roughly as in our text from p. 65 to Brown's exit a page later. Then the *Step* breaks off, the beggars gather round Peachum, and he makes them a long speech saying how much he has done for them. Pointing out how the rich cannot bear seeing people collapse from hunger because they are frightened that it might happen to them too—their one vulnerable point—he concludes 'Tomorrow will show whether poverty can overcome the crimes of those on top.' And '*the beggars feverishly start getting ready*'. End of scene.

Scene 8 [2 in script]

This corresponds to our optional scene, and it derives from Gay's Act 3 scenes 7 to 10. It starts thus, with the 'Lucy's Aria' whose setting by Weill is given as an appendix to the miniature score of 1972.

> *Newgate. Lucy's bedroom above the cells. Lucy is drinking non-stop.*
LUCY: Jealousy, Rage, Passion and Likewise Fear are tearing me to pieces, a prey to the raging tempest, tormented by worry! I have the Rats-bane ready. For the past day she has come here every hour wanting to speak with me. Oh, what a two-faced bitch! No doubt she wants to come and gloat at my desperation. O world! How evil the human race! But that lady doesn't know who she is dealing with. Drinking my gin is not going to help her have a high old time with her Mackie afterwards. She'll die thanks to my gin! It's here that I'd like to see her writhing! I rescue him from hanging, and is this creature to skim off the cream? Once that slut has drunk the poison, then let the world breathe freely!

Thereafter the dialogue generally follows Gay's (omitting his songs) down to Polly's 'I hear, my dear *Lucy*, our Husband is one of these.' Brecht then interpolates:

LUCY: I'll never be anything but a common trollop of the lowest sort. And
   why? Because I fail to put everything on a business footing.
POLLY: But my dear, that's a misfortune could occur to any woman.

They continue with the original dialogue, past Lucy's offer of the
drink, as far as her 'unless 'tis in private' in Gay's scene 10. Then Polly
excuses herself, saying she is hungry. The next passage is close to our
text from Polly '*gaily*' (p. 70) to Lucy's 'They've caught him once
more' just before the end of our scene, but with some small changes
and one or two additions, of which the most notable is after 'Really, I
don't deserve it' (p. 71):

LUCY: It's so unfair that one must use such means to keep a man; but it's
   one's heart, Polly. But enough of that.
   She takes the gin bottle and empties it, off.
POLLY: What are you doing?
LUCY *with a peculiar manner*: Emptying it.
POLLY: You really are a hypocritical strumpet. But I spotted that right away.
LUCY: Yes, Polly. On the edge of the precipice, that's where you were.
POLLY: Anyway it was very considerate of you. Here, have a sip of water.
   You must feel terrible. Why don't you come and see me. I truly am your
   friend.
LUCY: Polly, men aren't worth it . . .

There is then no change of scene, since the set is a split one, with the
bedroom above and Macheath's cell below. A change of lighting introduces our

Scene 9 [still 2 in script]

The bells ring, Smith leads in Macheath, and the dialogue is much as
in our text as far as Smith's exit shrugging his shoulders (p. 74).
Macheath then '*sings the "Epistle to his Friends" by François Villon*',
in other words our 'Call from the Grave', whose text is given. After its
second stanza Mrs Coaxer appears, and Macheath tries to borrow
£600 from her. 'What! At five in the morning?' she asks. Mac: 'Five?
He bellows: Five twenty-four!' Smith then puts his question about the
meal. Macheath says there isn't going to be a mounted messenger arriving like in a play to shout 'Halt, in the King's Name!' then tells
Smith: 'Asparagus!' Mrs Coaxer grumbles about her overheads, but
eventually agrees that she might be able to manage £400.
   Then the lights go up briefly in the bedroom again, showing Lucy

prostrate, with Polly giving her cold compresses. Enter Mrs Peachum, with Filch in attendance carrying a cardboard box. 'Go outside, Filch; this is not for your eyes,' she says, and tells Polly to get changed. 'You must do like all widows. Buy mourning and cheer up.' The bedroom darkens and the light returns to the cell, where Smith makes his inquiry about the soap (shifted from p. 74). After saying 'This place is a shambles' he brings in the table as on page 76, followed by Brown's entrance. The dialogue is then close to ours up to the end of Macheath's verse (p. 77). More persons in mourning enter, including Peachum and five beggars on crutches, while Brown and Macheath prolong their haggling over the former's percentages. Then Macheath looks at his watch and says '5.48. I'm lost'.

MAC: Jack, lend me £200. I'm finished. I must have those £200—for Polly, you know. 5.50. Here am I, talking . . .

BROWN *has come up to him:* But Mackie, you only have to . . . you only have to ask, you can right away . . . 500 right away—I owe you so much . . . Do you imagine I've forgotten Peshawar?

MAC *weakly:* 200, but right away. Right away, right away.

BROWN: And Saipong and Azerbaidjan and Sire, how we stood in the jungle together, shoulder to shoulder, and the Shiks mutinied, and you said . . . *The bells of Westminster interrupt him. Macheath gets up.*

MAC: Time is up. Jack, you're too emotional to rescue your friend. And you don't even know it.

Smith then opens the door, and a group including eight whores enters the cell.

Walter, with a little money-bag, stands near Macheath. Mrs Coaxer too has the money.

SMITH: Got it?

Mac shakes his head.

Peachum then asks which is Macheath, as in our text (p. 77), which thereafter is approximately followed down to (inclusive) Jenny's 'We Drury Lane girls . . .' (p. 78), but missing out the second half of Peachum's long speech (from 'Mr Macheath, you once . . .' to 'no place at all') and Matt's ensuing remarks ('See here' etc.). Brown too makes no more reference to Azerbaidjan but simply says farewell and leaves for the Coronation, gulping as he goes. Macheath's farewell speech follows, starting 'Farewell, Jackie. It was all right in the end' and going on with his 'Ladies and gentlemen . . .' as now, down to 'So

be it, I fall' (p. 79). As in Gay, however, it is Jemmy Twitcher who has
betrayed him, not Jenny.

The speech over, Macheath asks for the doors and windows all to be
opened, and '*Through the windows we see treetops crowded with
spectators*'. He then sings '*Ballad to his Friends by François Villon*',
whose text, however, is not given. After the ensuing farewells to Polly
and Lucy, Macheath is led to the door, the whores sob, and the procession forms behind him. Then:

> *The actor playing Macheath hesitates, turns round suddenly and
> doubtfully addresses the wings, right.*
>
> ACTOR PLAYING MACHEATH: Well, what happens now? Do I go off or
> not? That's something I'll need to know on the night.
>
> ACTOR PLAYING PEACHUM: I was telling the author only yesterday that
> it's a lot of nonsense, it's a heavy tragedy, not a decent musical.
>
> ACTRESS PLAYING MRS PEACHUM: I can't stand this hanging at the end.
>
> WINGS RIGHT, THE AUTHOR'S VOICE: That's how the play was written,
> and that's how it stays.
>
> MACHEATH: It stays that way, does it? Then act the lead yourself. Imper-
> tinence!
>
> AUTHOR: It's the plain truth: the man's hanged, of course he has to be
> hanged. I'm not making any compromises. If that's how it is in real life,
> then that's how it is on the stage. Right?
>
> MRS PEACHUM: Right.
>
> PEACHUM: Doesn't understand the first thing about the theatre. Plain
> truth, indeed.
>
> MACHEATH: Plain truth. That's a load of rubbish in the theatre. Plain
> truth is what happens when people run out of ideas. Do you suppose
> the audience here have paid eight marks to see plain truth? They paid
> their money *not* to see plain truth.
>
> PEACHUM: Well then, the ending had better be changed. You can't have
> the play end like that. I'm speaking in the name of the whole company
> when I say the play can't be performed as it is.
>
> AUTHOR: All right, then you gentlemen can clean up your own mess.
>
> MACHEATH: So we shall.
>
> PEACHUM: It'd be absurd if we couldn't find a first-rate dramatic ending
> to please all tastes.
>
> MRS PEACHUM: Right, then let's go back ten [?] speeches.

—and they go back to Macheath's 'So be it, I fall' once more. Then after the farewells to Polly and Lucy:

POLLY *weeping on his neck:* I didn't get a proper wedding with brides-
maids, but I've got this.

LUCY: Even if I'm not your wife, Mac . . .

MAC: My dear Lucy, my dear Polly, however things may have been between us it's all over now. Come on, Smith.

At this juncture Brown arrives in a panting hurry and his gala uniform.

BROWN *breathlessly:* Stop! A message from the Queen! Stop!

*Murmurs of 'Rhubarb' among the actors, with an occasional amazed
'From the Queen?'*

Then Brown calls for 'Bells!' into the wings, and makes his speech as
now (p. 81), adding at the end 'Where are the happy couples?'

MRS PEACHUM *nudges the others:* Happy couples!

*Whores, bandits and beggars pair off with some hesitation, choosing
their partners with care.*

Peachum thumps Macheath on the back and says 'It's all right, old
man!' Mrs Peachum speaks the last speech as now given to Peachum,
and the final chorale is given in full. After it Mrs Peachum has the concluding line: 'And now. To Westminster!'

3. FROM THE STAGE SCRIPT TO
THE PRESENT TEXT

The prompt book for the original production, which established the
greater part of the final text, is essentially a copy of the stage script just
discussed with new typescript passages interleaved, texts of songs, and
many cuts. It is now in the East German Academy of Arts in Berlin. At
the beginning there is a full text of the Mac the Knife ballad, only lacking its stage directions, while interleaved in the first Act are the 'No,
they can't' song, the Love Duet, the Finale and two verses of the Ballad
of Sexual Obsession. The version of Peachum's opening speech cited
above is deleted and replaced by ours; the speech presenting the types
of human misery also seems to have been added; and there is a fresh
version of the ending of the scene, starting from Filch's protest at washing his feet (p. 9), virtually as now. In the stable scene the start is retyped and the 'Bill Lawgen and Mary Syer' song pencilled in; the rest
emerges more or less in its final form, aside from the presentation of the

nuptial bed, which is still missing. Scene 3 seems to have been completely revised twice, the first time remaining close to the stage script, the second resulting almost in the text as now, apart from the section on p. 32 where Peachum apostrophises Macheath (which is also lacking where recapitulated in scene 9).

In the second Act an amendment to the end of scene 4 made the gang go out shouting 'Three cheers for Polly!' who then went on to sing 'Nice while it lasted' and continued with her monologue as in the stage script. This was then changed to give the complete text as now spoken over the music, from 'It's been such a short time' on. The song, of course, is all that remains of the second of the Kipling ballads, whose refrain it is; it was omitted from the song texts as published by Universal-Edition in 1928. The 'Ballad of Sexual Obsession', which follows in our text, is inserted before the beginning of the scene, but was omitted from the production and from the piano score of 1928. Scene 5, the brothel, was revised as far as the Villon song (or 'Tango Ballade'), but the setting remained the Cuttlefish Hotel; thereafter there were cuts. In scene 6 the only important additions were the text of the Jealousy Duet and Peachum's Egyptian police chief speech (p. 56–7), replacing the speech cited above in answer to Brown's 'What do you mean?'. The text of the second Act finale, too, was inserted just before the end of the scene.

In the third Act scene 7 was redesignated 'Peachum's Counting-House' and entirely revised; the additions included the 'Ballad of Insufficiency' (described as 'sung before the Sheriff of London') and the remaining verse of the 'Ballad of Sexual Obsession'. Brown's long speech about friendship was cut, also virtually everything following his exit. Though Lucy's Aria at the beginning of scene 8 was now cut out for good, the cut was not actually marked, perhaps because the whole of that scene was omitted from the production. Thereafter in the equivalent of our scene 9 Mrs Coaxer's appearance was cut, likewise most of the passage where Macheath tries to borrow money from Brown, down to Smith's opening of the door. What follows was retyped, again, however, omitting Peachum's apostrophising of Macheath (p. 77). Peachum's verse speech was interpolated and the Third Finale revised. The scene titles were separately listed, with instructions for their projection.

A later version of the Bloch stage script bore the title 'The Threepenny Opera (The "Beggar's Opera"). A play with music in a prologue and eight scenes from the English of John Gay', then gave the credits as before. The first published edition was number 3 of Brecht's Versuche series, which appeared in 1931 and described it as 'an experiment in epic theatre'. This contained the text as we now have it,

as also did the collected Malik edition of 1938. After the Second
World War, however, Brecht made certain revisions, notably for a
production at the Munich Kammerspiele by Hans Schweikart in
April 1949. For this he devised the amended song texts now given as
an appendix to the play, and made some small changes in the first Act,
eliminating for instance the entry of the five beggars in scene 3. He
discarded these improvements in the 1950s when it was decided to in-
clude the play in volume 3 of the new collected edition, for which he
went back to the *Versuche* text. The new songs, for instance, were not
used in Strehler's Milan production of 1956, though this included a
version of the final chorale which Brecht wrote for the occasion and
whose German text has been lost. A rough rendering would be:

> Since poverty won't haunt this earth for ever
> Don't blame the poor man too much for his sins
> But fight instead against perverted justice
> And may it be the human race that wins.

Mother Courage and Her Children

Penguin Classics proudly presents the authorized, definitive edition of Bertolt Brecht's masterwork *Mother Courage and Her Children,* with a foreword by Olympia Dukakis. This chronicle play of the Thirty Years War was Brecht's response to the ongoing horror of World War II. Following Mother Courage as she trails the armies across Europe, selling provisions from her canteen wagon while her children are devoured by violence, *Mother Courage and Her Children* is nothing less than a classic in the repertory of Western theater.

ISBN 978-0-14-310528-2